THE MOONSMITH

GULZAR

orbiting the celebrated words

Artist: Pintu Biswas

THE MOONSMITH

GULZAR

orbiting the celebrated words

SHAILJA CHANDRA

HAWAKAL PUBLISHERS PRIVATE LIMITED
70 B/9 Amritpuri, East of Kailash, New Delhi 65
33/1/2 K B Sarani, Mall Road, Calcutta 80

Email info@hawakal.com
Website www.hawakal.com

Cover photograph by Jitu Savlani

Cover designed by Bitan Chakraborty

First edition (paperback) November 2021

ISBN: 978-93-91431-21-1 (Paperback)

Price: INR 450 | USD 14.99

for

ma

and the departed souls of

papa, my mother-in-law, and father-in-law

CONTENTS

ORBITING THE MOONSMITH

All of us will endure existential angst at some point in our lives. Some of us will unearth our private rivers of pain and longings. And most of us will one day wake up to the pointlessness of everything — often not knowing how to reconcile with it all!

A multitude of writers, with their intellectual influences, might offer commandments to navigate our existential malaise. But only literary giants such as Gulzar offer spectacular persuasion and resonance that truly awakens us to a wholehearted and a 'high-resolution' life. He offers his own vulnerabilities, despairs and hopes via his words, rather than giving lofty ideals of how to live, love, and die. Because he is not opaque to himself, his words are piercing, redemptive — collective!

The premise of this book took roots in me right after my first meeting with Gulzar Saab in November 2012 for a radio interview. A momentous meeting when, seeping with a rare rawness of emotions and seasoned insights, his voice cascaded in me. It cut through my worldviews, gushed through the crevices of my soul, and carried parts of me into an abyss of longing.

2012 was also the year when I was churning within me with a deep desire to disentangle myself from who I thought I am. A year when I was vastly concerned with the futility and absurdity sitting at the core of the human condition.

Work on the book began in 2014 and, in the upcoming years, Gulzar Saab was to become the bearer of much of the weight of my existential angst. I was to orbit my guiding Moonsmith over and over again.

The book orbits Gulzar's writings on some of the greatest themes of existence. It is a homage to the way he writes about the intricacies of our inner lives, our inextricable connection with nature, and the inexplicable dimensions of our existence such as god, time, or death.

Through this book, I yearn to unravel how he rouses us to the majesty of the mundane that we neglect in our blind race to glorious destinations. How his words can cut through the 'frozen' within us — shifting us from exclusive to inclusive, and from numbly chasing elusive perfection to authentically embracing the fascinating fragilities within us.

I long to explore the resonant depths of Gulzar's voice on each subject — to distil the distinctive characteristics and essence where his signature poignancy, conscientiousness, or sagacity springs from.

I am extremely pleased and privileged to be able to share the 'captures' from my orbits in this book that — without attempting to demystify the enigma that Gulzar is — aims to offer fresh vantage points to unravel some unseen facets of some of the most celebrated words of the legendary poet.

If you cherish a deep bond with Gulzar Saab — the kind that is worn like a sacred *taweez* — and if you seek to verify life's dichotomies and other enduring questions of the human mind, this book will be of deep interest to you, as it offers new 'hooks' to recalibrate our realities, stretch our sensitivities and prod our perspectives.

I have also crystallised views of other writers and thinkers in my extensive research with a view to establish a correlation with Gulzar Saab's words, including Rabindranath Tagore, Khalil Gibran, Alan Watts, Henry Miller, Hannah Arendt, Carl Sagan, and many others.

The book also includes an exclusive conversation with Gulzar Saab — an antidote to my continued puzzlement about some of the complexities and challenges of modern humanity such as the inaction on climate change, human-hand in all this, and the pervasiveness of artificial intelligence and technology in our lives. His stronghold on the swiftly shifting sands of times is exactly what we need to hear to combat the growing culture of insecurities, excessive entitlements, and damaging apathy.

I was drawn to Gulzar Saab's words ever since I can remember, but in the early 90s this connection was to transform into an eternal 'gravitational pull.' If someone would have foreshadowed then, that decades later I would be able to meet him — let alone having the immense privilege of his valuable counsel in the writing of this book — I would have certainly dismissed it as a psychedelic fantasy.

But here I am, with a book that has been sanctified with a title presented by him.

Gulzar Saab would often read portions of my writings and convey his feedback despite a million things competing for his time. His words of encouragement and nuggets of advice would become my guiding light for many moons. But one remarkably transformative moment occurred in 2016 when, with many dreams and the 'final' manuscript in hands, I had visited him in *Boskiyana*. It was a day when my 'orbit path' was to change as Gulzar Saab told me in unambiguous words that the manuscript needed more work before it can be compiled into a book. He encouraged me to go beyond my comfort boundaries, advising me to write original thoughts and articles before compiling a collection. That day he forthrightly counselled me to not be hasty.

I returned to Sydney with full awareness of the rare privilege of hearing what would be the most important advice that a writer can ever receive, from none other than my Moonsmith!

In the following months, I reworked on the manuscript,

got two articles published at online literary magazines, and continued to seek his feedback. A defining moment came in 2018. During a phone conversation he said what I had always longed to hear — that he had noticed evolution in my words — that I could now start compiling the book. Such moments kept me forever enthused.

Gulzar Saab, thank you for the invaluable gift of your counsel, for seeing in me "the spark of a good writer," the seeds of "a big tree," and for conferring the title of 'surgeon' on me. I am extremely privileged! Thank you for your rare kindness — for sending me books that I was searching for my research, for checking on my father's health, endearingly asking 'is this a good time' at the start of every call — and for many more such heart-warming gestures. And for that momentous call on the 14th of December 2020 after reading the final manuscript — it will always reverberate in me! Thank you for your divine presence in my life. Thank you for your virtuous words — I shall eternally orbit them.

After thirteen years of corporate life in sustainability advisory, one day when my colleagues were huddling around my desk, wondering about my decision to resign to 'pursue my creative dreams,' little did I know then that the creative pursuit will be stumbling, humbling, yet deeply transformational and stunningly soul-stretching.

Along the path, I learned to practice unprotesting acceptance for the many bumps and derailings, including the trauma of seeing papa slowly disappearing and in less than four months of his prognosis, learning to be without him. A remarkable man and father, who always held immense pride and love for me in his heart — I wish he were here to hold this book in his hands.

I wish to thank my two loving brothers and sister and their families, and also families here in Sydney and the US — their love was always with me.

I must mention my radio-love Voice of India FM89.7. My first meeting (the 2012 radio interview) was an outcome of something I said to Vikram Sharma, the producer of the show: *Marungi nahin jab tak Gulzar Saab se na mil loon.* Thanks to him for making this elusive dream a reality!

Many thanks to my friend Manbir Kohli for wearing multiple hats — from being a great friend to a sounding board for my existential rants, and for connecting me to Kashiana Singh, who, with an earnest intent and rare swiftness, lead me to Hawakal Publishers. A big thanks to Kashiana — our *setu*!

A huge thanks to Kiriti Sengupta for a wonderful blend of calm and enthusiasm in his guiding voice, and for providing prompt and well-considered responses to my queries. Thank you for patiently leading me through the steps that got me here!

I wish to thank Pavan Jha for his reviews and support, and for always saying it like it is. Thanks to Ashok Bindal for his ongoing spirited support, and for *muskurahat aur khilkhilahat* along the way! Thanks also to Anil Mudgal, Atul Tiwari, Abhinav Upadhyay for their support.

Many thanks to John Zubrzycki for the very first review of grammar/syntax.

Thanks to my dear friends and well-wishers for their love and moral support — Jaya Singh, Sumit Malhotra, Arun Nanda, Ratna Kuppur, Renu Varshney, Chowdhurys and Sethis, Yvonne Lai, Graciela Magnoni, Avijit Sarkar and Rajpaul Sandhu.

In the stumbling and humbling journey of life, I will always have one guiding light of love, encouragement, and trust — and that is Samit, who cannot be acknowledged as he is inseparable to me. This book has been his dream more than mine.

Shailja Chandra
Sydney

GULZAR'S CONVERSATIONS WITH ERRATIC KHUDA

I have vivid recollections of a childhood dream in which *Shiva* was my playmate, helping me mend a torn kite on a sultry afternoon. 'Was I important in some way…?' The dream made me ponder for a long time.

In the coming decades, I will just be one of the billions of puppets in the one-sided game of rope-pulling — इक तरफ़ा रस्सा-कशी — without any influence to summon Him! Yet, that juvenile dream granted me certain childlike awe about the Supreme Being — preventing me from subscribing to any ritualistic mindset and also stopping me from turning into a nonbeliever.

I continued to wonder, seek, and surrender in equal measures and have discovered my own curiosity in Gulzar's inquisitiveness about God…

This wonderment spiked on 28th February 2020 as a car plunged on our local café, injuring eight of us and taking one life. Was someone 'watching over' me? Was it you my *playmate*? तू मुझे देख रहा है या नहीं, कोई इशारा तो दिखा. I survived with some injuries — to be grateful … and wonder about it all.

In Gulzar's intimate, forthright, and probing conversations with *Bade Miyan* — I find my own voice, my ongoing puzzlement and wonderment, and echoes of my connection with *Shiva* many dreams ago.

Orbiting the Moonsmith Gulzar revealed that, neither sombrely analytical nor like the Oracle's voice, Gulzar's writings on the nature of God carry a remarkable blend of candidness and clout and an acceptance for both our utter cosmic unimportance and the *Brahmand* in us. This chapter captures his all-rounded voice on this core preoccupation of the human mind.

"Why is God not female?" In April 2019, the Moonsmith spoke to this intriguing and unusual line of enquiry on the gender of God, sowing a fresh inquest about the topic. This conversation is enclosed at the end of the book.

Refreshingly conversational, playful, and forthright and at the same time carrying a charming blend of probing and seeking — Gulzar's voice on the nature of God effectively underscores the fertile, unfulfilled curiosity that mankind has always been grappling with:

बहुत से और भी सय्यारे हैं इस क़ायनात में
बदल कर देखें कोई और मालिक ज़िन्दगी का
कहीं पे और भी कोई ख़ुदा होगा! (*Pluto*, p 69)

जिस्म और जान टटोल कर देखें
ये पिटारी भी खोल कर देखें
टूटा फूटा अगर ख़ुदा निकले! (*Raat Pashmine Ki*, p 189)

This chapter visits the well-rounded discourse in Gulzar's writings about the nature of God that duly honours the complexity and mystery of a difficult subject. It highlights his unique receptivity and affinity with '*Bade Miyan*' and explores the essence behind the vigour and rigour of his voice on the subject. The three most prominent elements that this chapter explores are:

—The intimate, conversational voice, yet never without probing and seeking

—The exasperation in his voice about ritualistic mindsets — the hallmark of all organised religion that keeps losing its meaning and context with time

—And finally, the *sufi*-scientist in his voice that celebrates the mastery and mystery of the *Brahmand* with awe and wonderment, and claims significance in insignificance

INTIMATE, CANDID CONVERSATIONS WITH GOD

Neither analytical nor a tragic prophet-poet's voice but an intimate, conversational tone is what Gulzar embraces to engage with the subject of God and religion.

In his candid voice, I find it all — traces of probing, yearning for higher signs, and hints of scepticism or light-hearted accusations.

This unique blend makes for a well-rounded narrative on a complex and important subject. It is a voice in which readers easily find their own affinity, curiosity, and doubts about the nature of God and religion. It is a voice that refreshingly instigates an invigorating line of enquiry: that doubt can be more generative than jaded religious beliefs and stale faith systems.

It is a voice that appears to be Gulzar's unique way to make a private possession of an elusive God! ख़ुदा से कहिये, कभी वो भी अपने घर आयें!

ज़मीं भी उसकी, ज़मीं की ये नेमतें उसकी
ये सब उसी का है, घर भी, ये घर के बंदे भी
ख़ुदा से कहिये, कभी वो भी अपने घर आयें! (*Raat Pashmine Ki*, p 170)

मै जितनी भी ज़बाने जानता हूँ
वो सारी आज़माई है
ख़ुदा ने एक भी समझी नहीं अब तक
ना वो गर्दन हिलाता है, न हुंकार ही भरता है (*Paaji Nazmein*, p15)

जब धुआँ देता, लगातार पुजारी
घी जलाता है कयी तरह के छौंके देकर
एक जरा छींक ही दो तुम
तो यकीन आये की सब देख रहे हो (*Paaji Nazmein*, p14)

Owing to this intimate yet inquisitive tone, Gulzar can also remark on another complicated subject with incredible ease and impact. A subject that mankind has always grappled with. A subject that has always been difficult to write on without expressing anger, frustration, or without portraying God as a cold, malicious, and morally irresponsible being! This subject is God's apathy towards mankind and nature in times of calamities, riots, and other pitiful states — and the inexplicable unfairness and randomness of it all.

In a masterstroke, Gulzar defines God's apathy, mercurial nature, and His 'indulgence' in all the macabre surrounding mankind, as 'Erratic!'

बड़े 'इरैटिक' से लगते हो, काएनात में कैसे लोगों की सोहबत में रहते हो!

Here is an excerpt of this *nazm* where, without being solemn or accusatory, he reflects on the randomness of natural and man-made calamities and brilliantly substitutes the age-old, burdened question of 'Where is God in all this' with the mirthful काएनात में कैसे लोगों की सोहबत में रहते हो? — still instigating the much-needed enquiry laced with doubt and dissatisfaction:

पिछली बार मिला था जब मैं
एक भयानक जंग में कुछ मशरूफ़ थे तुम
नए नए हथियारों की रौनक़ से काफ़ी खुश लगते थे
इससे पहले अन्तुला में
भूख से मरते बच्चों की लाश दफ़्नाते देखा था
और एक बार ... एक और मुल्क में ज़लज़ला देखा
कुछ शहरों के शहर गिरा के दूसरी जानिब
लौट रहे थे...

बड़े 'इरैटिक' से लगते हो
काएनात में कैसे लोगों की सोहबत में रहते हो! (*Raat Pashmine Ki,* p 9)

Gulzar decides on the word 'erratic' to describe the indifference of God when a miracle is needed and when the winds and the earth are not obeying Him. I contemplate what happens when God is not just a bystander but appears to be actively indulging in the one-sided game of *karma*, *kismet,* and serendipity that mankind can never have a fair go at? Here is a selection of *nazms* where Gulzar expresses that helplessness:

उम्र के खेल मे इक तरफ़ा है ये रस्सा कशी
इक सिरा मुझ को दिया होता तो इक बात भी थी

मुझ से तगड़ा भी है और सामने आता भी नहीं' (*Raat Pashmine K*i, p 171)

नस्ले आदमी से कोई बदला लिया है तूने?
बादशाहों की तरह तुझको भी आदत तो नहीं ऐसे तमाशों की कहीं?
तेरे अंदाज़ मैं समझा ही नहीं हूँ शायद (*Pukhraj*, p 61)

वो अगरचे देखता है सब
उसपे ये कि आँख भी झपकता नहीं वो
सोचता हूँ मैं ही पर्दा कर लूँ अपने हुजरे पर
आसमां का टाट टांगकर!
क्यों मैं रोज़ रोज़ उसके नाम की सफ़ाई देता हूँ (*Pluto,* p 110)

Gulzar's conversations with God are indeed a significant part of our literary heritage — for his voice is not passive or solemn but always illuminating and shifting perspectives. Another characteristic of his voice on the nature of God is discussed in the next section.

DISCOMFORT WITH RITUALISTIC MINDSET

One subject where Gulzar adopts a more sombre tone and

displays unambiguous discomfort, and no mirth, is the matter of dated rituals and rubrics. Rituals that, in the form of organised religions, slowly risk losing their meaning and context for posterity. And rubrics that, in their harmful configurations, slowly turn into the biggest curses of organised religions — radicalism and misled zealots.

बिन पेंदा हैं नाम ख़ुदा के, उनमें अब ईमान नहीं भरता (*Neglected Poem*, p 130)

— so hard-hitting are Gulzar's exasperations on rituals and rubrics of religion that they seem to contain the seeds of a much-needed antidote to the curses of organised religions.

Trailing the same line of argument, he fervently voices the need for an expiry date for out-dated, baseless doctrine in an interview with Divya Marathi Network: अब धर्म का मामला दवाओं पर दी जाने वाली एक्सपायरी डेट की तरह है. तारीख़ निकल जाने के बाद दवा ज़हर की तरह होती है. इसलिए अब दवा बदलने का समय है. Indeed, the blind following of out-dated ritualistic structures of religious doctrines can be lethal. Similar sentiments are conveyed in the following *nazms*:

वो जो एक मीयाद थी ना
इस्तेमाल की —
वो गुज़र चुकी!! (*Neglected Poems*, p 132)

बुरा लगा तो होगा ए ख़ुदा तुझे, दुआ मे जब जम्हाई ले रहा था मैं —
दुआ के इस अमल से थक गया हूँ मैं!
मैं जब से देख सुन रहा हूँ तब से याद है मुझे,
ख़ुदा जला बुझा रहा है रात दिन,
ख़ुदा के हाथ में है सब बुरा भला ... दुआ करो!
अजीब सा अमल है ये, ये एक फ़र्ज़ी गुफ़्तगू
और एकतरफ़ा — एक ऐसे शख़्स से,
ख़्याल ही जिसकी शक़्ल है
ख़्याल ही सबूत है (*Raat Pashmine Ki*, p 7)

His views on the shortcomings of organised religion deeply resonate with the views of Alan Watts, namely that: 'Irrevocable commitment to any religion is not only intellectual suicide; it is positive unfaith because it closes the mind to any new vision of the world.' (*Alan Watts,* 1989)

In the following lines, Gulzar laments the growing banality of divinity — hinting and hitting at the decline and decay that mindless rituals can bring to a concept that should have remained profound, esoteric!

ख़ुदा बड़े क़दीम दौर की किताब है!
क़दीम दौर मे... हमेशा ऊंचे ताक पर पड़ी
रुमालों मे सम्भाल के रखी हुई किताब
चुने-से लोग पढ़ते सुनते थे उसे!
जदीद दौर मे ...
जदीद कोई इस्तेआरा भी नहीं
क्लिनिक के वेटिंग रूम मे, पुराने इक रिसोले की तरह
पड़ा हुआ है वो! (*Pluto,* p 67)

For a new vision of the world, we must doubt and probe our timeworn and deluded commitment to a religious ideology and its jaded beliefs. Gulzar's voice can navigate us to introspect such ritualistic mindsets and their inertness.

CELEBRATING SIGNIFICANCE IN INSIGNIFICANCE

What truly liberates Gulzar from the expectations of a believer and scepticism of a non-believer is his cosmic humility, and his deep awareness and comfort with the uncertainty, immensity, and immeasurability of things larger than us:

कितना छोटा है मिरा क़द
फर्श पर जैसे किसी हर्फ़ से इक नुक़्ता गिरा हो (*Pukhraj,* p 95)
कोई मद्दा है मेरी बात मे तो,
नून के नुक़्ते सी रह जायेगी 'ब्लॅक होल' से गुज़र के,
वो क्या समझेगा, मैं समझाऊँगा क्या? (*Raat Pashmine Ki,* p 4)

Beyond the bondage of rituals or rubrics, doubts or zeal, dissatisfactions, or questions — and relieving God from the endless duties to take care of our troubles and joys — Gulzar commits to the only eternal kinship that exists between the universe and humanity! That is: एक शख़्स, अकेला पूरी कायनात है पूरी universe है। पूरा ब्रह्मांड है आपके अंदर। Within and in everything around us. He grants me this *bhrmastra* during our 2012 Boskiyana tryst! (*Gulzar in conversation with Shailja Chandra,* 2012, *Boskiyana*)

Orbiting the Moonsmith, I also captured his cosmic humility about our utter cosmic unimportance and randomness: मैं बेमानी सा एक भटका हुआ पल हूँ ... लेकिन आपका वजूद तो है उस ब्रह्मांड के अंदर भी.

Whilst human beings appear to be here by a mere accident, a *beimaani* or a quirk, they carry in them the sanctity and vastness of the whole creation. This is how he describes this seemingly insignificant, random, yet momentous moment in human history in an interview — लेकिन वो लम्हा तो था, वो एक पल था तो सही.

> बेमानी से लम्हे — जब पूरे ब्रहमांड मे आपको अपनी हैसियत मालूम हो ना, जहां इतना कुछ होता है। ऐंवई सा गुज़रता हुआ लम्हा, जिसमे कुछ होता नहीं। लेकिन आपका वजूद तो है उस ब्रहमांड के अंदर भी। बिल्कुल उस तरह से जैसे ज़रा सी कालिख लग गयी उंगली पे, दूसरे पत्थर पर पोंछ दी। लेकिन वो लम्हा तो था, वो एक पल था तो सही।
> मैं बेमानी सा एक भटका हुआ पल हूँ...
> मैं ... काल से टूटता हूँ, और ना जुड़ता हूँ.
> पुराने मक़बरों से तुम कभी गुज़रो तो यूं करना
> दिया जलता था जिस आले मे, उस आले मे कुछ कालिख बची होगी
> ज़रा सा छू के उंगली पर उठा लेना, किसी पत्थर पर घिस के पोंछ देना
> (*Gyanodaya*)

ज़रा सा छू के कालिख उंगली पर उठा लेना, किसी पत्थर पर घिस के पोंछ देना — and thus Gulzar registers the absence of a presence. The presence of mankind that is fleeting, seemingly unimportant in the face of the infinite expanse of time and space. A presence that unceremoniously turns into an absence, yet it existed. And thereby, he ceremoniously reserves a deserving place in the universe. For himself, for mankind: लेकिन वो लम्हा तो था, वो एक पल था तो सही... आपका वजूद तो है उस ब्रहमांड के अंदर भी.

This is our significance in insignificance! The Creator, the *Brahmand*, is indeed indwelling in the complex and the simple; in creation, in nurturing, in evolution and destruction; in the sun and stone ... and in that shining speck of dust:

> ज़र्रा बनने के लिये कितनी सदियाँ जाती हैं जो सूरज को देख कर चमकता है...
> पत्थर बड़ा नहीं है, वो ज़र्रा बड़ा है सूरज मे चमका (*Gyanodaya*)

To disown our timeworn preconceptions about religion and God and to own our rightful place in the universe is an arduous quest. Gulzar's assertion of humanity's unique and important status within the universe — despite our triviality in it — is immensely empowering and inspiring for such a quest.

Gulzar's refreshing conversational voice, his voice against the ritualistic mindset, or the liberated voice of claiming significance in insignificance can pave new ways to doubt, investigate, or embrace the nature of God. His writings on God and religion are indeed important literary heritage for the continued evolution of humanity on a subject that demands urgent attention and examination.

In closing this chapter, here is *nazm Sardi Thi Aur Kohra Tha* in which, unpolluted from the vehemence of believers and verification of non-believers, Gulzar presents a tranquil imagery of the nature of God, carrying rare stillness and sanctity. Perhaps, it is in such a benevolent moment where divinity — Godliness — truly resides:

> सर्दी थी और कोहरा था
> और सुबह की बस आधी आंख खुली थी, आधी नींद में थी
> शिमला से जब नीचे आते

एक पहाड़ी के कोने में
बस्ते जितनी बस्ती थी इक, बटवे जितना मंदिर था
साथ लगी मस्ज़िद, वो भी लॉकेट जितनी
नींद भरी दो बाहें जैसे मस्ज़िद के मिनार,
गले में मंदिर के
दो मासूम ख़ुदा सोगे थे!
एक बूढ़े झरने के नीचे. (*Neglected Poem,* p 12)

GULZAR ON LOVE ... NOOR KI BOOND

Love is hypnotic in its beginnings…

"As you pulled the chair closer in that vintage café — owning the sun and the skies, stopping the breeze dead — I wondered how we always blissfully remain on the 'centre stage' of our attention until love 'casts' someone to replace us."

Love can be poignant in its endings…

"In a few moments, we will say final goodbyes and with that departing string of breath, I will stitch the 'not-knowing' to my heart — like a gash. Like an elixir!"

Love also beholds a middle that does not carry the same romantic ecstasy! As I scribbled this love story named 'Element Six,' I grappled to carry the same allure throughout — wondering about why love's virtues promise an inner wholeness of *panaah,* and why it can also bring pain and discontent.

At *Boskiyana*, I request the Moonsmith to peel-off the layers of '*tumhi se janmoo to shayad mujhe panaah mile*' from the *nazm Main* — yearning to trace the innate nature of love. What he says will also grant rare insights into the epic challenges of the middle — bridging the beginnings and the endings of love's journey:

"कोई भी emotion एक तरह से कभी नहीं रह सकता … It evolves. Every emotion evolves itself into the next emotion…"

My first ever cup of tea with my Moonsmith, I am in a trance — but I can lucidly hear the unequivocal realism in his voice. That day the creator of the heavenly love-ballad *Main* will also bring out the worldly dimension of love — stunningly upholding both its mysticism and pragmatism.

Orbiting the Moonsmith, I traversed his nuanced imagery on arguably the most primordial preoccupation of the human mind that, since time immemorial, has garnered much curiosity and awe. This chapter presents my captures.

> "Like many poets before me, I have searched for the perfect words to capture what love can mean. But if I succeed, perhaps then love itself will fail...for its very indescribable nature is what makes it both the thing we long for and the thing that torments us." (*Mathrubhumi,* 2018)

This is how Gulzar expressed his own awe about the nature of love. In his poetic quest for 'perfect words to capture' love, we get access to both — a raw freshness of emotions and seasoned insights about love. He upholds both its mysticism and pragmatism and expresses both its poetic pervasiveness and indescribability. He writes about it as 'the thing we long for' and also 'the thing that torments us'. And in between this, he grants some of the noblest and most nuanced imagery of love.

THE EVOLVING VIRTUES OF LOVE

Societies and cultures are highly prescriptive about how to love and what to feel when in love. This can set us up for disappointment unless we also embrace the less acknowledged and mutable parts of romantic love that do not carry the same glamour as its hypnotic beginnings and poignant endings do.

Parts that are equally, if not more, virtuous!

Gulzar's views on the innate nature of love are highly dignified because they are inclusive of its mutating parts also. Not only has he written elegantly about love's headiness, timelessness, and everlastingness, he has also duly acknowledged love's mundane, time-based, and evolving dimensions.

Gulzar shares rare insights into love's evolving virtues in what will remain the most heard and heeded segment of my 2012 radio conversation with him. Below is an excerpt:

> कोई भी emotion एक तरह से कभी नहीं रह सकता। It evolves. Every emotion evolves itself into the next emotion.

Speaking about the growth markings of love's natural evolution and mutations in the hands of time, he says:

> जब पहले पहल वो अच्छी लगी थी तो then you want to reach closer and you want to touch, *hai na*? You want to hold the hand and then आप voice लेके चले आये। फिर निगाहें लेके चले आये, फिर आप रोज़ मिलने लग गये, But then it becomes usual, *hai na*? Then the desire is to hold each other and — come let us get married, please let us! Sex gets into it. Sex is not an external experience. It is totally internal. That is when you are closest to the being of each other. But that also does not remain. It cannot become a habit. It germinates into a marriage, and marriage germinates into a child. And then your sharing starts with the child and growing up with the child, *hai na*? So, can you see how one emotion has evolved into so many and it has to go on and go on.
>
> (*Gulzar in conversation with Shailja Chandra,* 2012)

Without discriminating, he underlines that to mutate is as innate to love as being eternal and that in the many layers of its evolution, love gets preserved and cultivated.

With this, he expands our sense of love to a more nuanced and multifaceted level. The kind that the ancient Greek philosophy identifies that there are many kinds of love within love, each evolving into another. The headiness of love's beginnings is *Eros*, which evolves into *Philia* — a love of two equals collaborating and growing together. Then there is *Agape*, the tender-hearted love and unconditional surrender to someone's imperfections and fragilities.

In *Boskiyana*, I am in a daze hearing him speak on the evolving virtues of love and this elegant dimension of total surrender:

> Your beloved is sometimes just like a mother to you and sometimes like a child. क्या बचपना करते हो, प्यार भी करते हैं आप, आंसू भी पोंछ देते हैं, नाक भी पोंछ देते हैं। Like a child. And there are times when you just put your head into her lap and hold her and you want to say — काश मैं तुमसे पैदा हुआ होता. Like a mother to me. So, it's an experience of that total surrender — a total giving in to your love. कि तुम्हारी कोख से जन्मू तो शायद पनाह मिले, शायद टहराव मेरे मे आये.
>
> वतन मिला तो गली के लिए भटकता रहा
> गली में घर का निशान ढूंढता रहा बरसों
> तुम्हारी रूह में अब, जिस्म में भटकता हूँ
>
> लबों से चूम लो, आँखों से थाम लो मुझको
> तुम्हारी कोख से जन्मूँ तो फिर पनाह मिले (*Pukhraj,* p 30)

His reading of *tumhi se janmoo to shayad mujhe panaah mile* that day is a pilgrimage in love, where he unveils that it is in total surrender where the ultimate mooring or *panaah* of love can be earned, not in its labels. Gulzar's imagery on this core virtue of love is explored separately in the next section.

PANAAH IN SURRENDER — A CORE VIRTUE OF LOVE

Love lives not in the resting depths of fulfilment, or ownerships. Rather its vitality springs from being in a state of longing and surrender, just as a river earns its strength by remaining in the perennial flow! Underlining this, the highly virtuous allegories of *nadiya* (river) and *behna* (inflow) find a vital place in Gulzar's expression of love:

बहने दे, मुझे बहने दे
बहने दे घनघोर घटा,
बहने दे पानी की तरह
सागर में जा गिरना है,
बहने दे नदिया की तरह
बह जा, बह जा, है सागर का कहना
बह जा, बह जा, है नदिया को बहना (*Raavan,* 2010 Film)

न ये बुझती है न रुकती है न ठहरी है कहीं
नूर की बूँद है सदियों से बहा करती है (*Khamoshi,* 1969 Film)

To be in flow is to surrender to love's course. Becoming acquisitive and directorial can only strangulate the perennial flow of its celestial *Noor*. Guarding the purity of emotions and experiences, he said the following in an interview:

> क्षण को कोई बांध नहीं पाया, ना स्पर्श को थाम पाया है. फिर उनके बेवजह कोई नाम देकर अंजाम की क़ैद मे घुटता हुआ क्यों छोड़ें? ग़म गूंगा है, एहसास बेनाम. वे सब मे हैं, पर किसी के नहीं. उसे पा सकते हैं, पर देख नहीं सकते. उन्हे अपना बनाने के रिवाज़ के कटहरे मे क्यों खड़ा करे कोई? (*Interview with Ruma Sengupta*)

Similar sentiments resonate in these lines also:

हमने देखी है उन आँखों की महकती ख़ुशबू
हाथ से छू के इसे रिश्तों का इलज़ाम ना दो
सिर्फ़ एहसास है ये रूह से महसूस करो,
प्यार को प्यार ही रहने दो कोई नाम न दो (*Khamoshi,* 1969, Film)

In my impressionable years, every time the timeless ballad *Humne Dekhi Hai Un Ankhon* played on the radio, it conveyed a 'code' or an immutable truth as Gulzar reminded us of love's innate nature to abound like the eternal drop of divinity, and to let it stay untouched, unlimited and unlabelled.

Decades later in *Boskiyana*, I hear him speak on the elegant dimension of total surrender, not as a philosophy but as a poignant account shared in a raw voice that knows no ownerships, only surrender:

> — काश मैं तुमसे पैदा हुआ होता … Like a mother to me. So, it is an experience of that total surrender — a total giving in to your love. कि तुम्हारी कोख से जन्मू तो शायद पनाह मिले, शायद ठहराव मेरे मे आये… (*Gulzar in conversation with Shailja Chandra,* 2012).

Nazm Main is a poetic embodiment of love's virtues. With potent allegories such as *kokh and panaah,* it carries intricate allusions that make it a textbook of sorts of love!

…लबों से चूम लो, आँखों से थाम लो मुझको
तुम्हारी कोख से जन्मूँ तो फिर पनाह मिले (*Pukhraj,* p30)

The *nazm* is a proclamation of the moment when someone else truly embraces us with all our failings, follies, and our unappealing and disgraced aspects. Or awakens us to our dormant, deeply hidden depths that lay within us — waiting to be unearthed. It is 'an experience of that total surrender, a total giving in to your love,' as the Moonsmith says in unravelling the *nazm.*

In all its allusions, love's *panaah* is a sense of redemption that can be experienced only in total surrender and not in our fallible tendency to assign labels and acquisitions. This is the alchemy of love!

मैं क़ायनात में, सय्यारों में भटकता था
धुंए में धूल में उलझी हुई किरण की तरह
मैं इस ज़मीं पे भटकता रहा हूँ सदियों तक
गिरा है वक़्त से कट के जो लम्हा, उसकी तरह ...

... लबों से चूम लो, आँखों से थाम लो मुझको
तुम्हारी कोख से जन्मूँ तो फिर पनाह मिले (*Pukhraj*, p30)

I am reminded of Gibran's "Think not you can direct the course of love, for love, if it finds you worthy, directs your course." Indeed, love's *panaah* in *Main* is ethereal, enigmatic, and entrancing like a *Sufi's* prophecy!

Gulzar has portrayed love as a virtue that can transcend the human experiences and touch the mind-expanding limitlessness — making the world, well, *less* worldly, more divine!

At the same time, in his many portrayals love also makes the world *more* worldly by bringing habituating patterns of comfort to make sense of the disorienting limitlessness.

In the last section, we explore this fascinating pair of complementing dimensions and another all-embracing outlook on love by Gulzar.

LOVE MAKES THE WORLD BOTH LESS AND MORE WORLDLY

In many of his writings on love's seeded magic, Gulzar enables a heavenly experience of love. Less dense — more transcendental! It is an experience that surpasses the five senses and the traditional concepts of space and time. It is an experience of a *pilpila* pulsating moment such as this:

दो सौंधे सौंधे से जिस्म जिस वक़्त, एक मुट्ठी में सो रहे थे
लबों की मद्धम तवील सरगोशियों में साँसें उलझ गयी थीं
मूंदे हुए साहिलों पे जैसे कहीं बहुत दूर ठंडा सावन बरस रहा —
बस एक ही रूह जागती थी

बता तो उरा वक़्त गैं कहाँ था ?
बता तो उस वक़्त तू कहाँ था? (*Pukhraj*, p 51)

I have picked selected imagery below where Gulzar's portrayal of love makes the world *less* worldly — transcending the limiting dimensions and touching the limitlessness of the moment:

1)Where love halts the eternal flow of time, or it collapses the eternity of three billion years to something trivial. Less worldly, more cosmic:

ख़त्म हो जाता है जैसे वक़्त का लम्बा सफ़र
तैरती रहती है इक गुंचे के होटों पे कहीं
एक बस निथरी हुई शबनम की बूँद

तेरे होटों का बस इक लम्स-ए-तवील
तेरी बाँहों की बस एक संदली गिरह (*Pukhraj*, Page 130)

कितनी देर लगा दी तुमने आने में
और अब मिलकर किस दुनिया की दुनियादारी सोच रही हो
...किस मज़हब और ज़ात और पात की फ़िक्र लगी है
आओ चलें अब
तीन ही 'बिलयन' साल बचे हैं! (*Pukhraj*, Page 51)

2) Or where love elevates us to a higher, finer dimension — endowing us with an experience of our own godliness:

वो एक लम्हा बड़ा मुक़द्दस था जिसमे तुम जन्म ले रही थी,

वो एक लम्हा बड़ा मुक़द्दस था जिसमे मैं जन्म ले रहा था
ये एक लम्हा बड़ा मुक़द्दस है, जिसको हम जन्म दे रहे हैं

खुदा ने ऐसे ही एक लम्हे मे सोचा होगा,
हयात तख़लीक़ करके लम्हे के लम्स को जाविदां भी कर दें
(*Pukhraj*, p 120)

तुम्हारे हाथों को चूमकर , छूके अपनी आँखों से आज मैंने
जो आयतें पढ़ नहीं सका उनके लम्स महसूस कर लिए हैं
(*Pukhraj*, p 121)

तिरे लबों पे ज़बान रखकर
मैं नूर का वो हसीं क़तरा भी पी गया हूँ
जो तेरी उजली धुली हुई रूह से फिसलकर तिरे लबों पर ठहर गया था
(*Pukhraj*, p 55)

3) And where love liberates us from the mortal burdens of the sensory body — to something limitless and sublime:

तुम्हारी बाँहों में डूबकर ऐसे हल्का-हल्का लग रहा है
कि जिस्म से जैसे सैकड़ों जिस्म उतर गए हैं
कि रूह से जैसे जिस्म का बोझ हट गया है (*Pukhraj*, p 33)

हथेलियों में अभी तलक तेरे नरम चेहरे का लम्स ऐसे छलक रहा है
की जैसे सुबह को ओक में भर लिया हो मैंने
बस एक मद्धम सी रौशनी मेरे हाथों-पैरों में बह रही है
(*Pukhraj*, p 55)

As I orbited his imagery on love, it came as a spectacular revelation that Gulzar has written equally of love's human dimensions also where it manifests as an earthly (not divine), comforting (not heady), orienting (not mystifying) compass to make sense of the expansive limitlessness around us. Making the world, well, *more* worldly! As Carl Sagan said, "for small creatures such as we, the vastness is bearable only through love":

ऐसे बिखरे हैं रात दिन जैसे
मोतियों वाला हार टूट गया

तुम ने मुझको पिरो के रखा था (*Raat Pashmine Ki,* p 190)

सिरे उधड़ गए हैं सुबह-ओ-शाम के
वो मेरे दो जहान साथ ले गया (*Raat Pashmine Ki,* p 156)

पनाह मिल जाए रूह को जिसका हाथ छूकर
उसी हथेली पे घर बना लो (*Pukhraj,* p 13)

ये पहली नवंबर की ख़बरें हैं सारी
निज़ामे-जहाँ इस तरह चल रहा है
मगर ये ख़बर तो कहीं भी नहीं है,
कि तुम मुझसे नाराज़ बैठी हुई हो —
निज़ामे-जहाँ किस तरह चल रहा है? (*Raat Pahmine Ki,* p 56)

Blending the insights of a poetic scientist and the alchemy of a mystic, Gulzar indeed is an important literary voice on love — unveiling its many complementing and enigmatic layers: That every emotion evolves and diverges into many tributaries yet all it gains is more vitality; that there is mooring in surrendering to love; that love is timeless, luminous *Noor*, yet it mutates; and that love can bestow a sense of divine limitlessness and also bring habituating patterns of comfort...

In closing the chapter, here is an excerpt from *Takhleeq* underlining how his nuanced outlook on love springs at the confluence of earthly and ethereal, of eternal and evolving — and of *rooh* and *jism*!

मैं अपने होटों से चुन रहा हूँ तुम्हारी सांसों की आयतों को
कि जिस्म के इस हसीं काबे पे रूह सजदे बिछा रही है
(*Pukhraj,* p 120)

GULZAR – THE JULAHA OF THE LIBAAS OF RELATIONSHIPS

"In this world, there are only two tragedies. One is not getting what one wants, and the other is getting it." Oscar Wilde said in a cruel and heartbreaking reflection that eloquently speaks to both the allure and the curse of love and relationships.

They continue to care for each other — perhaps more — after a separation creates a chasm between two people. A legal mechanism can grant them divorce but cannot take away the residual belongingness. The law is only paper-thin — it cannot pierce the inner layers of a relationship.

I call it the '*Tere Bina*' conundrum when it is not as simple as not being in love. Where living together ceases to be an option but living apart is equally heartbreaking.

Every time I witness two people in this conundrum, I marvel at the brevity of these two lines penned in the 70s. What initiated a life-long love with Gulzar, this song also became the centrepiece of one of my articles.

तेरे बिना ज़िन्दगी से कोई शिकवा तो नहीं
तेरे बिना ज़िन्दगी भी लेकिन ज़िन्दगी तो नहीं

What grants him a monopoly in portraying relationships in an unabridged manner ... showing all the markings and knots of mistakes and regrets, and the slow degeneration of the '*libaas*' of a relationship?

At Boskiyana, the Moonsmith describes how he accesses a panorama of emotions that lie outside the girth of his personal experiences:

आपके रिश्तों की तहें आपके चारों तरफ बिखरी हुई हैं। आपकी अपनी, sensitivities है, sensibilities हैं, कि आप दूसरों को कितना महसूस कर सकते हैं।

The antennas of his unique sentience and sensibilities to feel others have unquestionably granted us some of the most iconic and immutable truths on the intricate nature of relationships — with an instantaneous personal connection and collective healing. This chapter captures them.

तेरे उतारे हुए दिन टंगे हैं लॉन में अब तक

Why do we continue to belong to bygone times and relationships? Why does our sense of belongingness not wither as rapidly as the withering relationship?

Why do we uphold our egos with fervour and loyalty, and why does the revival of waning relations prove to be challenging?

Gulzar weaves the *taana-baana* of such intricate nature of relationships like a skilful *julaha*:

मेरे कपड़ों मे टंगा है, तेरा खुशरंग लिबास
घर पे धोता हूँ मैं हर बार उसे, और सुखाकर फिर से ...
अपने हाथों से उसे इस्त्री करता हूँ मगर
इस्त्री करने से जाती नहीं शिकने इसकी
और धोने से गिले शिकवों के चिकत्ते नहीं मिटते!'
(*Raat Pashmine Ki*, p 147)

This chapter explores Gulzar's writings on the poignant and heartbreaking realities of the mutating nature of relationships — on how the gaping chasms of separation create an endless pit for the cold-damp ego and resentments to seep deep, but how it might also create the perfect gradient for love to flow.

This chapter can be considered a continuation of his writings on love's innate nature, but it unveils a heart-rending dimension where the subtle layers of two souls and bodies are afflicted by a withering relationship:

हर इक शय में गयी उड़ती हुई, जलती हुई किर्चें
नज़र में, बात में, लहज़े में,
सोच और सांस के अंदरI
लहू होना था इक रिश्ते का, सो वो हो गया
उस दिन! (*Raat Pashmine Ki*, p 74)

CONFLUENCE OF EGO, POWERLESSNESS AND INCOMPLETENESS

These intricately intertwined sentiments of separation seem to blend seamlessly and heartachingly in Gulzar's writings on separation:

The bitterness of unresolved egos that divide, though the bond of love and care still unites...

The deep longing to bring back the bygone, though the unpleasant memories often torment...

The deflating sense of incompleteness, though life goes on living...

It is the confluence of these where the poignancy of many of his poems springs from. This truly delineates Gulzar's writings on relationships:

रात भर जो मिला उगते बदन पर हमको
काट के डाल दिया जलते अलाव में उसे
रात भर फूँकों से हर लौ को जगाये रखा
और दो जिस्मों के ईंधन को जलाये रखा
रात भर बुझते हुए रिश्ते को तापा हमने (*Pukhraj*, p 43)

Gulzar captures the subtle shades of these intertwined sentiments with such poetic authenticity that the aching silences between two love-torn souls speak volumes of pain, and the devastatingly raw '*wabi-sabi*' of nostalgias asks for full access to our souls:

मैने जेबों से निकाली सभी सूखी नज़्मे
तुम ने भी हाथों से मुर्झाये हुए ख़त खोले
अपनी इन आँखों से मैने कई मंज़र तोड़े
और हाथों से कई बासी लकीरें फेंकी
तुम ने, पलकों पे नमी सूख गयी थी, सो गिरा दी (*Pukhraj*, p 43)

बहुत फूंका सुलगते चाँद को, फिर भी उसे
इक इक कला घटते हुए देखा
बहुत खींचा समन्दर को मगर साहिल तलक
हम ला नहीं पाये ,
सहर के वक़्त फिर उतरे हुए साहिल पे
इक डूबा हुआ ख़ाली समन्दर था!! (*Raat Pashmine Ki*, p 84)

Selected *nazms* are excerpted below to convey how Gulzar weaves a poignant blend of these sentiments of separation:

1) His deeply moving reflections on how two people can uphold their unresolved egos with the same fervour and loyalty with which they love:

इश्क़ में लाज़मी हैं, हिज्रो-विसाल मगर
इक अना भी तो है, चुभ जाती है पहलू बदलने में कभी
रात भर पीठ लगाकर भी तो सोया नहीं जाता (*Pluto*, p 20)

बड़ी वफ़ा से निभायी तुमने
हमारी थोड़ी सी बेवफ़ाई (*Thodi Si Bewafai*, 1980 Film)

हाथ भर के फ़ासले को उम्र भर चलना पड़ा (*Yaar Julahe*, p 116)

2) On the deep longing to bring back the bygone, though the unpleasant memories may often return to torment and former times may never return:

मज़ार पर खोल के गरेबान दुआएं मांगे
जो आये अबके तो लौट के फिर ना जाए कोई
दिखाई देते हैं धुंध में जैसे साये कोई
मगर बुलाने से वक़्त लौटे ना आये कोई (*Yaar Julahe*, p 146)

तमाम रात-दिन यहीं पे रुकते हैं
बदल के पहलू, फिर से बात तुम्हारी जारी रखते हैं!
ये शाम एक वक़्फ़ा है (*Pluto*, p 47)

सावन के कुछ भीगे-भीगे दिन रक्खे हैं
और मेरे इक ख़त में लिपटी रात पड़ी है
वो रात बुझा दो (*Ijaazat*, 1980 Film)

ख़ुशबू गुंचे तलाश करती है
बीते रिश्ते तलाश करती है (*Visaal*, 2001)

3) And then there is that sense of heart-aching incompleteness — of how life irrevocably ceases to have 'life' in it while the perpetual cyclic workings of the world continue to roll, and the schema of things may appear unchanged:

सब कुछ वैसा ही चलता है
जैसे चलता था जब तुम थी
रात भी वैसे ही सर मूंदे आती है
दिन भी वैसे ही आँखें मलता जागता है
तारे सारी रात जमाइयां लेते हैं (*Neglected Poems*, p 94)

... ये पहली नवंबर की ख़बरें हैं सारी
निज़ामे-जहाँ इस तरह चल रहा है
मगर ये ख़बरें तो कहीं भी नहीं है की
तुम मुझसे नाराज़ बैठी हुई हो —
निज़ामे-जहाँ किस तरह चल रहा है? (*Raat Pahmine Ki*, p 56)

तेरे जाने से कुछ तो बदला नहीं
सांस भी वैसे ही चलती है हमेशा की तरह
आँख वैसे ही झपकती है हमेशा की तरह
थोड़ी सी भीगी हुई रहती है और कुछ भी नहीं

तेरे बिना ज़िन्दगी से कोई शिकवा तो नहीं
तेरे बिना ज़िन्दगी भी लेकिन ज़िन्दगी तो नहीं (*Aandhi*, 1975, Film)

Amidst these intertwined sentiments of separation also shines Gulzar's poignant reflection that unrealised longings may well become slow fuel to keep a connection kindled — reflecting Rebecca Sonnit's (2006) sentiment that 'Some things we have only as long as they remain lost, some things are not lost only so long as they are distant':

शहद जीने का मिला करता है थोड़ा थोड़ा
जाने वालों के लिए दिल नहीं थोड़ा करते (*Yaar Julahe*, p 150)

तुम्हारे ग़म की डली उठाकर,
ज़ुबां पर रख ली है देखों मैंने
वो कतरा-कतरा पिघल रही है
मैं कतरा-कतरा ही जी रहा हूँ (*Pukhraj*, p 91)

The next section discusses the recurring presence in his writings of the bond of love and care that continues to live and breathe long after a relationship has perished.

PERISHABILITY OF RELATIONSHIPS VS. PERMANENCE OF LOVE

A recurring theme in Gulzar's writings is the presence of residual 'deep roots' of a relationship that prove hard to remove. In such reflection he has beautifully brought out the contrast between the perishability of relations vs. the permanence of bond of love:

तेरे उतारे हुए दिन टंगे हैं लॉन में अब तक
न वो पुराने हुए, न उनका रंग उतरा
कहीं से कोई भी सीवन अभी नहीं उधड़ी (*Neglected Poems*, p 44)

The artful repetition of iconic allegories, such as 'days that hang unchanged in the lawn or *aangan'* and reference to 'roots that run deep', are reflective of Gulzar's constant awareness of the bond of love that gets matted and muted into the depths of the relationship. And so intricately that even *Siddharth*, the *Buddha*, could not free himself of the bond:

हर सम्बन्ध बंधा होता है,
दोनों सिरों से,
इक सिरा तो खोल गया था,
दूसरा खुलवाना बाकी था —
शायद उस मन की गिरह को, खोलने
लौट के आया हूँ मैं! (*Raat Pashmine Ki*, p 72)

What is equally anguishing is that the depth and breadth of the roots are revealed only when it is uprooted — as Khalil Gibran reflected: 'Man cannot reap love until after sad and revealing separation...'

सारे बाग़ीचे में फैली हुई निकली हैं जड़ें ,
बरसों पाले हुए रिश्ते की तरह
जिसकी शाखें तो हरी रहती हैं, लेकिन
उस पर, फूल फल आते नहीं (*Pukhraj*, p 85)

What is spectacular about Gulzar's imagery and intricate details of the many layers of separations is that it is not just about the perishability of the bed, bills, and bolts of relationships — but also about the permanence and agelessness of the bond of love that lives in the 'deep roots' and 'unchanging days' that can never be pulled out. Just like E.M. Forster (1908) said: "You can transmute love, ignore it, muddle it, but you can never pull it out of you."

मैं शब को कैसे बतलाऊँ,
बहुत से दिन मेरे आँगन में यूँ आधे अधूरे से
कफ़न ओढ़े पड़े हैं कितने सालों से,
जिन्हे मैं आज तक दफ़ना नहीं पाया!! (*Raat Pashmine Ki*, p 64)

जहाँ से तुम मोड़ मुड़ गए थे, वो मोड़ अब भी वहीँ पड़े हैं
हम अपने पैरों में जाने कितने भंवर लपेटे हुए खड़े हैं
(*Thodi Si Bewafai*, 1980 Film)

मैं चुप करता हूँ हर शब उमड़ती बारिश को,
मगर ये रोज़ गयी बात छेड़ देती है

तेरे उतारे हुए दिन पहन के अब भी मैं
तेरी महक में कई रोज़ काट देता हूं!! (*Neglected Poems*, p 44)

एक अकेली छतरी में जब आधे-आधे भीग रहे थे
आधे सूखे, आधे गीले, सूखा तो मैं ले आई थी
गीला मन शायद बिस्तर के पास पड़ा हो
वो भिजवा दो, मेरा वो सामान लौटा दो (*Ijaazat*, 1987 Film)

Indeed, the constant presence of the deep-rooted, unchanged bond of love and care — rather than its perishability — is the more pronounced undertone of his poetry on relationships and separation. And it is this bond that no legal mechanism can take away or grant to a relationship:

आओ, अब उठ जाएं दोनों
कोई कचहरी का खूंटा दो इंसानों को
दस्तरख़्वान पे कब तक बाँध के रख सकता है
क़ानूनी मोहरों से कब रुकते हैं, या कटते हैं रिश्ते
रिश्ते राशन कार्ड नहीं हैं!! (*Neglected Poems*, p 48)

It is this bond of care and love that is 'more than enough.' In his words: 'You still care. That's what keeps us together even today and that's more than enough...'

हाथ छूटें भी तो रिश्ते नहीं छोड़ा करते (*Yaar Julahe*, p 150)

SYMBOLS OF UNIVERSAL RESONANCE

Gulzar's motifs and symbols on relationships are undoubtedly some of his most iconic and powerful works — touching the eloquence and simplicity of folk wisdom and conveying universal insights into human relations.

His iconic motifs and symbols match the earthiness and raw verve of homespun immutable truth of *Kabir* and *Rahim,* including his iconic poetic lament to *Yaar Julaahe.* Selected allegories are shared below:

वक़्त को जितना गूंध सके हम,
गूंध लिया (*Neglected Poems*, p 48)

सम्बन्ध भरा इक थाल गिरा था —
गूँज हुई थी, लेकिन मैं ही वो आवाज़
फलाँग आया था —
हर सम्बन्ध बंधा होता है,
दोनों सिरों से,
इक सिरा तो खोल गया था,
दूसरा खुलवाना बाकी था —
शायद उस मन की गिरह को, खोलने
लौट के आया हूँ मैं! (*Raat Pashmine Ki*, p 72)

मुझको भी तरकीब सिखा यार जुलाहे
अकसर तुझको देखा है कि ताना बुनते
जब कोई तागा टूट गया या ख़त्म हुआ
फिर से बांध के
और सिरा कोई जोड़ के उसमे
आगे बुनने लगते हो
तेरे इस ताने में लेकिन

इक भी गांठ गिरह बुनतर की
देख नहीं सकता है कोई
मैंने तो इक बार बुना था एक ही रिश्ता
लेकिन उसकी सारी गिरहें
साफ़ नज़र आती हैं मेरे यार जुलाहे (*Yaar Julahe*, p 43)

...ज़िन्दगी किस क़दर आसां होती
रिश्ते गर होते लिबास —
और बदल लेते कमीज़ों की तरह! (*Raat Pashmine Ki*, p 147)

What grants Gulzar a monopoly in portraying human relations in an unabridged and universal manner is this elegant blend of his creative and emotional forthrightness — the way he marks the 'knots' or the *girhen* of mistakes, vulnerabilities, repentance, and slow degeneration of the '*libaas*' of a relationship:

मैंने तो इक बार बुना था एक ही रिश्ता
लेकिन उसकी सारी गिरहें
साफ़ नज़र आती हैं मेरे यार जुलाहे (*Yaar Julahe*, p 43)

इस्त्री करने से जाती नहीं शिकने इसकी
और धोने से गिले शिकवों के चिकत्ते नहीं मिटते! (*Raat Pashmine Ki*, p 147)

While it may be convenient to see the emotional authenticity in his writings as chronicles of his own '*aap-beeti*', however, the creative process of a virtuous writer can never be this easily observable!

Sitting in his sacred presence, I ask the Moonsmith about his rare dexterity and emotional authenticity to present the finest nuances of relationships, their evolution and decay: ऐसा लगता है की जो आप लिख रहे हैं, आप उस से गुज़र चुके हैं, आपने वो महसूस किया होगा, आपके साथ ऐसा हुआ है, इसलिये ये नज़्मों मे आ रहा है। What part of your writing is a reflection of you — the pain, the complexities, the sensitivities of relationships?

This is how he elaborates on his creative process:

> सारा कुछ ख़ुद आप-बीती नहीं होती। लेकिन आपकी जो observation है, किसी भूखे को देख कर जो महसूस किया मैने — that becomes my आपबीती। वो एहसास जो मेरे अन्दर उतरा है उसे देख के, वो मेरा हिस्सा बन गया है। वो सिर्फ बाहर नहीं रह गया ... It is not something, which happened to you. It is something to which you reacted as it happened to others. You internalise their experiences.
>
> ...कहीं ना कहीं आप की observation है कहीं ना कहीं आप का experience है। लेकिन आप शामिल ज़रूर हैं उस creativity मे जो आपने लिखा है।
>
> क्योंकि आप जितने relations मे ख़ुद गुज़रते हैं, उनकी layers उसके बाहर भी हैं। अगर मैने तलाक़ नहीं दिया बीवी को, तो मेरी बहन को जो तलाक़ देके चला गया क्या वो महसूस नहीं हुआ मुझे? आपके रिश्तों की तहें आपके चारों तरफ बिखरी हुई हैं। आपकी अपनी sensitivities है, sensibilities हैं, कि आप दूसरों को कितना महसूस कर सकते हैं।
>
> (*Gulzar in conversation with Shailja Chandra*, 2012)

His unique sentience and sensibilities to feel others allow him to access a panorama of emotions that lie outside the girth of his personal experiences, and then to internalise them. This is how Gulzar makes an instantaneous individual connection and brings universal sagacity and collective healing. Indeed, Gulzar has written the '*taana-baana*' of the intricate nature of relationships like a skilful *julaha*!

> ....मैंने तो इक बार बुना था एक ही रिश्ता
> लेकिन उसकी सारी गिरहें
> साफ़ नज़र आती हैं मेरे यार जुलाहे (*Yaar Julahe*, p 43)

GULZAR ON THE AAINA OF TRUTH AND REALITY

Subconsciously and subtly, we keep adding flawed 'spellings' of our emotional and behavioural patterns, and unfounded biases to 'the dictionary' of life. The 'autocorrect' then starts to write our life — binding us to our limited mental cages and chastising us to repeat the old patterns of ignorance.

At Boskiyana, I am waiting with wide-eyed awe to hear his views on how to combat such subtle influences and deceptions. But before sharing his remarkable perspectives on truths of life that continue to reveal new layers with each listen every passing year, my Moonsmith adds a disclaimer, "ज़िंदगी एक सी तो होती नहीं, इसलिये किसी के पास कोई final word तो नहीं है कि ज़िंदगी यही है।"

He gives this liberating truth that day and more immutable *mantras* such as below — vital to release us from the self-inflicted cages of our unfounded yet steadfast opinions:

अगर पूरी कायनात आपकी, पूरा globe आपका घूमता फिरता है, तो आपको घूमने की आदत डाल लेनी चाहिये, and not fix yourself.

A few years later, I am privileged to uncover more layers of truth-seeking as he speaks about 'becoming a cave' by throwing ourselves — our delusions and the overgrown jungle of knowledge — out of us.

Gulzar is an unmatched mentor anyone can have in the quest for life's truths. He brings out what is most enduring and true in a moment. The privilege of his enriching mentoring is a rare treasure of my life — vital for recalibrating my worldviews and my inner world.

While orbiting the Moonsmith Gulzar, I collected his compelling imagery that shakes us from our 'wakeful sleep', and reminders on how to find new 'frames' and 'hooks' of imagination and how not to evade facing our fears and flaws. This chapter captures them.

अच्छे भले थे, पूरे थे हर बात में मगर
आईने में देखा तो, दो टुकड़े हो गए

यहीं पे माथों की रौशनी जल के बुझ गयी है
सपाट चेहरों के खाली पन्ने खुले हुए हैं
हुरूफ़ आँखों के मिट चुके हैं

मैं खंडहरों की ज़मीन पे कब से भटक रहा हूँ
यहीं कहीं ज़िन्दगी के मानी गिरे है और गिरके खो गए हैं (*Yaar Julaahe*, p 76)

There has been impenetrable mongering of wars, lies, greed since the time immemorial by the pervasive demagogues of media, organised religions, and regimes. They continue to create deceptive smoke and mirrors — masking all traces of truth and reality. And the 'soot' that gradually settles on our minds proves to be difficult to pierce and purge.

Despite how implausible unbridling the truth may seem, the intent that we assign to its quest is vital to a wholehearted existence.

In Gulzar's writings, there is unequivocal significance assigned to the quest — to the process of 'bit by bit seizing of the curtains', and to pierce the smoke and mirrors and purge the delusive 'soot'.

This chapter discusses Moonsmith Gulzar's powerful allegories and writings that characterise the quest for truth and reality. Mainly two dimensions of this quest are discussed:

combating imperceptible influences and combating deceptive inner delusions.

COMBATING IMPERCEPTIBLE EXTERNAL INFLUENCES

Our perspectives of truth and reality become stale and partial with the slow and deep osmosis of various external influences. Growing deeper and impenetrable, these influences transcend many folds of time, countless generations, and numerous institutions — be they cultural, educational, religious, or familial. As Gulzar says:

अपनी मर्ज़ी से तो मज़हब भी नहीं उसने चुना था (*Yaar Julaahe*, p 84)

Indeed, our most internal emotions may not be our own but 'borrowed' from others. The following lines appear to be alluding to such layers of external influences that shape us:

ख़्याल, सांस, नज़र, सोच, खोलकर दे दो
लबों से बोल उतरो, ज़ुबाँ से आवाज़ें
हथेलियों से लकीरें उतारकर दे दो
हाँ, दे दो अपनी 'ख़ुदी' भी की 'ख़ुद' नहीं हो तुम ... (*Pukhraj*, p 90)

मेरी नादानियाँ भी मेरी नहीं
पूछ लो उनसे जो बड़े हैं यहाँ (*Yaar Julaahe*, p 153)

Our minds become so constricted with hidden biases and distorted facts that even our worldviews on some of the most important and plagued issues of our times, such as misguided jingoism or jaded religious intolerance are not truly our own.

It all becomes even more complex when these distortions are not coerced but wilful. The following lines seems to be referring to our wakeful sleep or the 'cages' that we wilfully choose:

कई पिंजरों का क़ैदी हूँ...
कई पिंजरों में बसता हूँ
मुझे भाता है क़ैदें काटना
और अपनी मर्ज़ी से चुनाव करते रहना
अपने पिंजरों का...
मैं क़ैदी हूँ (*Neglected Poems*, p 50)

Whether it is combating our wilful blindness, comfort 'cages', or recalibrating the damaging shift in our worldviews — a sense of meaning springs from stumbling and in the noble act of overcoming them elegantly.

Gulzar reminds us that vital to this stumbling and the seizing of curtains from truth is to cultivate open-mindedness and not focusing so tightly that we leave out something important. Gulzar refers to it as:

ख़्याल को कभी चैन न दिया, stagnant नहीं होने दिया

The following *nazm* captures this alertness of thought:

बदल के देखें तो रस्ता,
वहीँ से आते-जाते हैं हमेशा!
बहुत से और भी सय्यारें हैं इस क़ायनात में
बदल कर देखें कोई और मालिक ज़िन्दगी का
कहीं पे और कोई भी ख़ुदा होगा! (*Pluto*, p 69)

Exhibiting the same quality of thought-vigilance, he offers new 'frames' and 'hooks' of imagination in the following *nazm* — for the 'triangulation' of facts and to speculate beyond accepted knowledge and boundaries to reach the furthest fringes of reality and truth:

जी चाहे कि
पत्थर मार के सूरज टुकड़े-टुकड़े कर दूँ
सारे फ़लक पर बिखरा दूँ इस काँच के टुकड़े

जी चाहे की
लम्बी एक कमंद बनाकर
दूर उफ़क पर हुक लगाऊँ
खींच के चादर चीर दूँ सर से
झाँक के देखूं पीछे क्या है

शायद कोई और फ़लक हो (*Pukhraj*, p 93)

Inspiring us to be open to new horizons and evidence, here Gulzar's words merge with Terje Toftenes: 'Maybe there are concepts of our reality we have yet to understand, and if we open our eyes maybe we will see that something significant has been overlooked.'

This underlines another virtue — vital for the quest for truth — that Gulzar spoke to me about. It is the virtue of intellectual humility, of knowing that the certitude of being right or wrong does not apply to the quest:

अब ऐसा नहीं है कि मैं जो बोल रहा हूँ वो मैं सब जानता ही हूँ और सब सही है। है ना...। ये तलाश रहती है जानने की।

During our 2012 *Boskiyana* conversation, I ask him about his views on making mistakes and being wrong. His words are like oxygen to the breathless:

आप ना बिल्कुल सही हैं, ना बिल्कुल ग़लत हैं। बल्कि एक process मे भी हैं सीखने के। So, a mistake is just a part of the process of making you. आपकी बनावट का हिस्सा है ग़लती। उसे अलग कर के खींच के मत देखिये — वो उसी दीवार मे fit होगी। वो ज़रूरी है। वो breathing के लिये ज़रूरी है।

Exhibiting a rare intellectual and existential humility, Gulzar says:

...ऐसा नहीं है कि जो आप ने सोचा बस वही है। There are others

> also. और जो सब सोचते हैं वो आप नहीं हैं। तो in a way you are finding or gaining another vision of life.
>
> ...ये मुमकिन नहीं है कि जो मैं सोचता हूँ, सब वैसा ही सोचेंगे। और ये भी मुमकिन नहीं कि जो सब सोचे, मैं वही सोचूं। So, it's an equation, और वो extend होती रहती है। मतलब हम तो दुनिया को जान भी कहाँ पाये हैं। कितना ही जाना है ?
>
> इस globe का जो size है, 300 ज़मीने एक Jupiter मे आ सकती हैं। और कल की जो खबर थी that they have found another planet around another star, which can accommodate 300 Jupiter. तो अगर ये है, तो आपकी हद कहाँ खींचेंगे आप?

In our 2019 conversation, Gulzar shares that intellectual humility has been a vital pillar of Carl Sagan's scientific and philosophical enquiries:

> Human beings are limited in their thinking because they can only think up to a certain extent. जो सोच रहें हैं वो आपकी इस genetic growth में possible है. Only then you can think of it.

Intellectual humility is about acknowledging that we cannot possibly know the hidden infinites of truth. It is about embracing the unknowns and the ever-evolving nature of our existence.

Liberating us from the burden of finding immutable and objective truth and echoing Gibran's "Say not, I have found the truth, but rather, I have found a truth," Gulzar affirms:

> अगर पूरी कायनात आपकी, पूरा globe आपका घूमता फिरता है, तो आपको घूमने की आदत डाल लेनी चाहिये, and not fix yourself.

He further adds: Horizon तब हो कि साहिब जो नज़र में आ रहा है that is the end. But it is not so. You start travelling towards the horizon, so is it the same spot? The horizon keeps on extending further — वो fix नहीं हो सकता and that is the evolution. That is the evolution of society. That is the evolution of human beings.

कुछ भी क़ायम नहीं है, कुछ भी नहीं
और जो क़ायम है, बस इक मैं हूँ

मैं जो पल पल बदलता रहता हूँ (*Pukhraj*, p 47)

वक़्त रहता नहीं कहीं टिक कर
इसकी आदत भी आदमी सी है (*Yaar Julahe*, p 162)

Everything is in a flux and the horizon is ever-evolving, we can still be 'truth-scientists' and work towards completing the incompleteness of what we see, hear, and perceive. We can still 'cease to cherish opinions.' (*A Zen saying)*

This elegant pairing of exploration and humility is what makes Gulzar's writings greatly persuasive on how to pierce through the impenetrable layers of the deceptive smoke and mirrors.

झाँक के देखूं पीछे क्या है
शायद कोई और फ़लक हो (*Pukhraj*, p 93)

The next section explores his writings on the second dimension of the 'bit-by-bit seizing of curtains': our deceptive inner illusions.

COMBATING DECEPTIVE INNER ILLUSIONS

'Truth can be uncovered only through self-knowledge'
(Jiddu Krishnamurthy)

Eckhard Tolle in his powerful book *A New Earth* writes: '"I" embodies the primordial error, a misperception of who you are...This illusory self then becomes the basis for all further interpretations or rather misinterpretations of reality...The good news is: If you can recognise illusion as illusion, it dissolves.'

Gulzar puts an uncomfortable mirror to our faces with his powerful allegories of *aaina* and *chehra* (mirror and face). These two allegories are immensely potent in diagnosing our imperceptible ignorance (and arrogance) that result in naive-realism and delusional self-righteousness:

हैं नहीं जो दिखाई देता है
आईने पर छपा हुआ चेहरा

तरजुमा आईने का ठीक नहीं (*Raat Pashmine Ki*, p 191)

The allegory of aaina represents not just self-introspection but also self-confrontation. In these lines, Gulzar invites us to take a hard look at our inner self, challenging the construct of who we falsely believe we are and aiding in dissolving inner illusions:

अच्छे भले थे, पूरे थे हर बात में मगर
आईने में देखा तो, दो टुकड़े हो गए (*Chamak Calendar*)

कोई ऐसा गिरा है नज़र से कि बस
हम ने सूरत न देखी फिर आईने की (*Yaar Julahe*, p 167)

How can we combat our tendencies to conveniently edit out information or to admit only what aligns with our familiar beliefs? How can we challenge the constructs of our ego that fiercely protects itself from any damage? Consider the *nazm* below that compels us to look at such 'blind-spots':

मैं जब भी गुज़रा इस आईने से,
इस आईने ने कुतर लिया कोई हिस्सा मेरा।
इस आईने ने कभी मेरा पूरा अक्स वापस
नहीं किया है —
छुपा लिया मेरा कोई पहलू ,
दिखा दिया कोई ज़ाविया ऐसा,
जिस से मुझको, मेरा कोई ऐब दिख ना पाये ।
मैं खुद को देता रहूँ तसल्ली
कि मुझ सा तो दूसरा नहीं है !! (*Raat Pashmine Ki*, p 42)

This *nazm* is a brilliant take on our tendency to remain narrowly concerned with our dressed-up inner truth and a false sense of self-righteousness — how we evade owning our own shadow. The following *Triveni* alludes to the same:

आओ सारे पहन लें आईने
सारे देखेंगे अपना ही चेहरा

सबको सारे हसीं लगेंगे यहां (*Raat Pashmine Ki*, p 167)

To add to the layers, Gulzar also acknowledges the coexistence of good and bad within us in this rare reflection:

> Every human personality has many faces. There are compartments which open or close. Like when you turn the lights on or off, only a particular area is lit or drowned in darkness. (*As quoted in Kaghaz*)

In the following lines, he prepares us to be valiant about acknowledging these blends of 'shades' in human nature:

एक भी हैं अनेक भी आदम
एक चेहरे में कितने चेहरे हैं (*Pukhraj*, p 137)

जिस्म के खोल के अंदर ढूंढ रहा हूँ और कोई
एक जो मैं हूँ, एक जो कोई और चमकता है

एक मयान में दो तलवारें कैसे रहती हैं (*Raat Pashmine Ki*, p 193)

मैंने एक साया अपना पाल रक्खा है
आगे पीछे घूमता है जैसे छोटा टॉमी है
भौंकता नहीं कभी किसी भी अजनबी पे ये
अपना ही मिले कोई तो काट लेता है
साया मेरा काट ले तो दांत के निशाँ छोड़ देता है
मैंने अपना ज़हर सब साये में संभाल रखा है
मैंने एक साया अपना पाल रक्खा है (*Collage*, August 2015)

Unless we acknowledge this 'blend' — of the complexity and duality within us — the reality will remain fragmented and partial as these lines indicate:

कोई सूरत भी मुझे पूरी नज़र आती नहीं
आँख के शीशे मेरे चुटख़े हुए हैं कब से

टुकड़ों टुकड़ों में सभी लोग मिलें हैं मुझ को (*Raat Pashmine Ki*, p 183)

Gulzar's allegory of *aaina* — a symbol of pure presence without the residue of our biases and conditioning — is immensely potent. Such a distortion-free *aaina* — although elusive — is indispensable to the quest of truth and reality, and to transcend us beyond our falsehoods.

In closing this chapter, it must be reiterated that while we may be able to combat some of the delusions and deceptions bit by bit, seeking absolute truth is highly unrealistic.

There is perhaps something closer to the subtlety and purity of truth. It occurs 'when writers make us shake our heads with the exactness of their prose and their truths.' (*Anne Lamott,* 1995).

Describing Gulzar's ability to summon beauty and truth, Dr. Dharmveer Bharti wrote in *Gulzar — Ek Shakshiyat*, 'बुद्धि और दर्शन के माध्यम से आदमी सिर्फ सच्चाई के बाहरी दायरे तक पहुँच पाता है — सच्चाई को मुसलसल पाने का रास्ता ह्रदय का रास्ता है, भावनाओं का रास्ता है।'

Here is *nazm, Mariam,* through which Gulzar transports us beyond the divide of truth and lies — giving us glimpses of the 'absolute' amidst a relative world, gazing right into the numinous-luminous reflections of purity. *Mariam* is perhaps a rare experience of truth accessible to mankind!

रात में देखो झील का चेहरा
किस क़दर पाक, पुरसुकूँ, ग़मगीं
कोई साया नहीं है पानी पर
कोई सिलवट नहीं हैं आँखों में
नींद आ जाये दर्द को जैसे
जैसे मरियम उदास बैठी हो
जैसे चेहरा हटाके चेहरे का
सिर्फ एहसास रख दिया हो वहाँ (*Pukhraj*, p 94)

THE MONA LISA EFFECT IN GULZAR'S WRITINGS ON SOIL & SOCIETY

The day was rapidly setting in Sydney's economic center, yet the design workshop had not resolved on my appeal to save the six native trees and the ancient life in them.

Most had started packing up but the architect and me. With his spectacles resting precariously on his nose and eyes glued to the details offered on my last slide of the day, he whispered: 'Trees...are like great solitary men, like Beethoven ... and Nietzsche' (Words of Hermann Hesse). Aware of everyone's gaze, he cleared his throat nervously, 'I'll review the design. We may be able to find a way to save some of the trees.'

No collective consensus, collaboration, or deliberation could have rescued those trees. Nothing can be as powerful as a private moment of realisation, belongingness, and a sincere pledge — the kind we find in Gulzar's voice on our soil and society.

Whether it is on the pathos of the environment, our society, or any other socio-political issues of our *daur*, his words convey deeply personal moments of vulnerability and belongingness, not dry impersonal social commentary:

मोड़ पे देखा है वह बूढ़ा-सा इक पेड़ कभी? मेरा वाक़िफ़ है, बहुत सालों से
मैं उसे जानता हूँ...

Some years later in April 2019 at *Boskiyana*, my Moonsmith takes me on another privileged pilgrimage into the sentient 'subconscious' of nature and how it senses the infringing footprints of road-rollers and other construction vehicles:

...और वो ये भी जानते हैं कि ये पगडण्डी इतनी चौड़ी हो गयी है और हमें रोड-रोलर्स की आवाज़ें आने लगी हैं, कटने के दिन क़रीब हैं, कटने के दिन क़रीब हैं... उन पेड़ों को पता है...

Orbiting the Moonsmith allows fresh vantage points to admire the rare authenticity, persuasiveness, and virtuosity of his voice on our soil and society. This chapter takes it up.

Khalil Gibran said: "Every beauty and greatness in this world is created by a single thought or emotion inside a man."

Gulzar's work on the soil, society and our moral, environmental, ethical recklessness is a treasure trove of such potent, poignant 'single thoughts and emotions.' Words that convey intense, personal moments of belongingness — not impersonal social activism:

मोड़ पे देखा है वह बूढ़ा-सा इक पेड़ कभी ?
मेरा वाक़िफ़ है, बहुत सालों से मैं उसे जानता हूँ...
... सुबह से काट रहे हैं वह कमेटी वाले
मोड़ तक जाने की हिम्मत नहीं होती मुझको (*Green Poems*, p 24)

At no point does his voice put a contemptuous mirror to social decadence. Nor does it ever issue dry precepts of reform or sing ballads of mutiny from an ivory tower. Instead, with deep sentience, he speaks of the raw tales of the scars, spirit, and struggles of the soil and society. Here is one such struggle of asphalt-concrete longing for a small chunk of the sky:

पत्थर पे पत्थर रख रख के
एक मकां ऊपर उठने की कोशिश में है
साथ की छत पे कुहनी रख के
आसमान का कोई कोना देख सके! (*Green Poems*, p 58)

What makes his voice on the soil and society so passionate, personal, and persuasive? This chapter explores this.

THE ETERNAL NATIVE IN HIS VOICE

Kakadu National Park located in Australia's Northern Territory is a uniquely vibrant place that allows an instant connection with its rich cultural and spiritual heritage through Australian indigenous folklores called the Dreamtime Stories.

I am fascinated by the Dreamtime Stories that are not just conduits between the ancient laws, wisdom and values and later generations but also powerful prayers of the indigenous communities since time immemorial: Prayers to pay their deep respects and to show affinity to the scattered footprints of the spiritual ancestors on its timeless soil — the trees, the billabongs, rocks, land, and the animals:

> *We belong to the ground*
> *It is our power and we must stay close to it or maybe*
> *We will get lost.* (*Australian Dreaming,* p 99)

A similar sense of foresight, respect and belongingness with nature flows in Gulzar's sentient voice in 'मोड़ पे देखा है वह बूढ़ा-सा इक पेड़ कभी? मेरा वाक़िफ़ है, बहुत सालों से मैं उसे जानता हूँ' or 'हमीं से हो ... हमीं में फिर से बोए जाओगे, तुम फिर से लौटोगे' or 'मैं जंगल से गुज़रता हूँ तो लगता है मेरे पुरखे खड़े हैं'...

Just as the Dreamtime Stories of the *Bininj* and *Mungguy* natives reflect in the ancient billabong of Yellow Waters, Gulzar's voice resonates in us with immense potency — invoking a sense of affinity and custodianship in us. Like a native folksong, it connects us to the immutable ancient laws of nature and brings us 'home' — to the forgotten truth:

> मैं जंगल से गुज़रता हूँ तो लगता है मेरे पुरखे खड़े हैं
> मैं इक नौ ज़ाइदा बच्चा

ये पेड़ों के कबीले
उठ के हाथ में मुझ को झुलाते हैं (*Green Poems*, p 14)

पहाड़ों से बिछड़ कर लौटता हूँ तो
कई दिन तक उतरता रहता हूँ उनसे
ख़ला में लटका रहता हूँ
कहीं पांव नहीं पड़ते! (*Green Poems*, p 36)

The true essence of his 'native' voice rests in his unmatched ability to pour his own vulnerabilities, anguish, and despairs into it. Whether he is contemplating about environmental degradation, social decadence, or the heartbreaking state of communal riots, his method is of confronting his own reality, not of criticising; of discovering his personal truth, not impersonal perspectives; of compassion, not of uprising:

जंगल से गुज़रते थे तो कभी बस्ती भी कहीं मिल जाती थी
अब बस्ती में कोई पेड़ नज़र आ जाएं तो जी भर आता है
दीवार पे सब्ज़ा देख के अब याद आता है, पहले जंगल था (*Yaar Julahe*, p 125)

The ability to share vulnerabilities lends his voice rare authenticity and persuasiveness. It bestows him a rare authority to write on our shared existence, our *Sanjha Rishta*.

जब तक मेरे सामने वाले घर की बत्ती जलती है, उस घर की सारी परछाइयाँ मेरी दीवार पर पड़ती है — हमारा रिश्ता तो वैसा है...साँझा रिश्ता है ।

In an interview, when the suggestion was made that his method for liberation rests in individuality, the anguish was evident in Gulzar's voice:

कैसे? Individuality में कैसे? मैं जलते शहर में बैठा शायर इस से ज़्यादा करे भी क्या? जब वो कहता है तो वो पूरे शहर की बात कर रहा है — तो वो अकेला रास्ता नहीं ढूंढ रहा है. अकेले के लिए, वो पूरे समाज की बात कर रहा है ... ख़ून देख कर टाप के दूर हो जाता हूँ... नौ-ग्यारह

> की गाड़ी पकड़नी है । मैं ऐसा बेहिस हुआ हूँ...” मैं अपने अकेले की बात तो नहीं कर रहा हूँ — मैं उस पूरे समाज की बात कर रहा हूँ जिसे मैं देख रहा हूँ । (*Rajya Sabha TV*, 2012)

I had to rewind this part many times and the question that continued to spool on my mind was: Writing with intimacy and writing about the collective — are these mutually exclusive?

On my way to *Boskiyana* in 2012, I knew that this must be on the top of my list — the topic of collective Vs. individual:

क्या मुक्ति अकेले नहीं पायी जा सकती? I ask him.

> हम्म ... अकेले भी पायी जा सकती है, और आपके साथ जो जुड़ जाएं उन्हे भी मिल जायेगी। हैं ना? ... हाँ ... वो इतना अकेला नहीं है, इतना अकेला भी नहीं है।

Indeed, it is an intriguing paradox that the more intimacy and vulnerability Gulzar imbues his words with, the more universal and collective his voice becomes. No, they are not mutually exclusive!

> ख़ून देख कर टाप के दूर हो जाता हूँ...
> नौ-ग्यारह की गाड़ी पकड़नी है...
> मैं ऐसा बेहिस हुआ हूँ.

A private, intimate reflection such as this is indeed the genesis of any meaningful kinship with the collective. Without perceiving the pain on a personal level, it is not possible to write authentically about the collective. Without this, only shallow pity or preaching can be expressed, not the sensibility and sentience these lines carry:

> कुएं के आस पास अब कुछ नहीं है
> ज़रा से फ़ासले पर इक पुराना पेड़ जामुन का
> अब उस पर फल नहीं आते...

वो तो कह गयी थी, फिर से लौटेगी
मैं छोड़े हुए कुएं की मानिंद वहीँ ठहरा हुआ हूँ
उतरने लग गया हूँ
ख़ुश्क होता जा रहा हूँ! (*Green Poems*, p 66)

Only a native voice can be without shallow pity or preaching. Only a native voice can ennoble and dignify shared existence. Such a 'native' eternally dwells in Gulzar's voice.

LENDING VOICE TO THE UNSEEN AND THE UNHEARD

Autumn colors surround my street for several weeks between May and July. In those weeks, I find Gulzar's imagery everywhere — on the auburn branches and the fallen ochre-bronze foliage. Not even the real living-breathing-falling leaves feel as alive, vibrant, and fecund as his words:

ख़िज़ां झाड़न लिए पत्ते गिराती फिर रही है क्यों दरख़्तों से
ख़िज़ां को क्या हुआ है?
वो बौराई हुई फिरती है जैसे पीले पत्तों पर लिखी कोई इबारत है
मिटाना चाहती है (*Green Poems*, p 106)

The autumn with a duster in hand and the ancestral jungles; the aged rivers and those rowdy clouds; the magician earth and September's allergic sky; or February's frost and the ageing tree at the crossroads — each of these spirited portrayals by Gulzar seem to carry nature's own fecund life-energy and its healing and transformational capacity.

His imagery, just like nature, is fresh, fertile, unbound — never stale. We feel as invigorated by his words as we feel amidst the mist of *Sanobars* or soaking in the sonorous sound of an exuberant *dariya.*

वक़्त ने अपना रुख बदला और...
परबत परबत पाँव रखता नीचे उतरा

रात की गोद में शाम पड़ी थी
दरिया लिपटा हुआ खड़ा था पीपल से
और पहाड़ के सीने पर, पहली-पहली घास उगी थी! (*Neglected Poems*, p 30)

धुंधले-धुंधले
ड्राइंग बुक में बने हुए कुछ चारकोल की ख़ाके से
कोहरे में किरदार ये पेड़ों के कितने अच्छे लगते हैं...
...आर के लक्ष्मण के कार्टूनों के किरदार
शायद उड़ कर झाड़ियों में जा अटके हैं
हवा का झोंका छूता है तो रोल बदल जाते हैं इन किरदारों के
पोशाकें बदल कर लौट आते हैं (*Green Poems*, p 28)

I long to reach out and touch the maiden ground cover on the broad torso of that mountain and my time-constrained train journey to work is enlivened and deepened by meeting R.K. Laxman's cartoons in the bushes of Lane Cove National Park...

His anthropomorphic work is a truly distinctive and remarkable treatise for the collective. His imagery is not merely about humanising nature, trees, and valleys in charming, spirited characters. His intricate and piercing attention also unveils unseen-unheard-untouched dimensions of the many imperceptible phenomena of nature. And for this, his imagery feels whole, real!

The qualities that truly separate Gulzar's voice from other anthropomorphic works appear to be a result of the following:

1) He can perceive nature's cycles coinciding with the cycles of life, day, night; or how imperceptibly, subtly nature's soul and body change with the cycles of seasonality:

दरख़्त सोचते हैं जब, तो फूल आते हैं
वो धूप में डुबो के उँगलियाँ
ख़्याल लिखते हैं, लचकती शाख़ों पर
तो रंग रंग लफ्ज़ चुनते हैं
ख़ुशबुओं से बोलते हैं और बुलाते हैं (*Green Poems*, p 18)

2) He perceives not just the spirited state of the muted members of nature but in deep silence he also listens to the restless rustles and ripples of the trees and the rivers — touching the eternal truth and trust in the ancient laws of life that they stand for, tall and deep:

ख़िज़ां दरवाज़े के बाहर खड़ी थी
अभी पोशाक से पत्ता कोई उधड़ा नहीं था
सुनहरी सुर्ख होने लग गए थे ज़र्द पत्ते
सभी के कान 'गौतम बुद्ध' के जैसे लंबे लंबे
बस इक आवाज़ के सब मुन्तज़िर थे
'चलो अब छोडो शाखें,
त्याग दो बंधन
सबा लेकर निजात अब आ रही है!! (*Green Poems*, p 104)

3) He whispers to their vulnerabilities, scars, and their inner-most fears and turmoil when their flows collide with the growth-cycles of the developing civilisation:

रात की ख़ामोशी में लेकिन थंपू छू
कुछ जाप किया करती हो तुम
वो क्या है?
सागर संगम कहती हो या
फेंटे जाने से बचने की —
चुपचाप दुआएं करती हो? (*Green Poems*, p 26)

बड़ी उदास है वादी
गला दबाया हुआ है किसी ने ऊँगली से
ये सांस लेती रहे, पर ये सांस ले न सके! (*Raat Pashmine Ki*, p 75)

पता चलता है कि पर्वत परेशां हैं!
बड़े नाराज़ लगते हैं वो जब अपनी चट्टानों को
उठा कर खंदकों में फेंक देते हैं !
ज़मीं हिलती है जब पांव पटखते हैं ।
उन्हें अच्छा नहीं लगता,

सुरंगे खोद के सीने में उनके
जब कोई बारूद के गोले उड़ाता है!! (*Raat Pashmine Ki*, p 110)

कुआँ बंद हो रहा था
कुएं की सांस घुटती जा रही थी...
...परों को फड़फड़ा कर उसके पानी में नहाती थी
परेशां थी...
बड़ी बेचैन थी पीपल पे उड़ती फ़ाख़्ता दिन भर
परेशां थी कि, इक ज़िंदा कुएं को लोग क्यों दफ़ना रहे थे!! (*Green Poems*, p 64)

Can the pathos of the *Thimpu Chuu* River find a more poignant and persuasive voice than this, and *Wadi-e-Kashmir*?

Gulzar's humanising portrayals have earned him a rare authenticity and authority to remind humanity to reinstate nature's role as the tribal head, the eternal teacher, or as the ancient custodian of the truth and values — just like the reminder in these lines:

मेरे सनोबर देखो कितने ऊंचे ऊंचे क़द हैं उनके
तुम से सात गुना तो होंगे
उम्रें देखो उसकी तुम, कितनी बड़ी हैं (सदियों ज़िंदा रहते हैं)
कह देते हो कहने को तुम
लेकिन अपने बड़ों की इज़्ज़त करते नहीं तुम
(इसलिए तुम लोगों के क़द ... इतने छोटे रह जाते हैं) (*Green Poems*, p 128)

THE MONA LISA EFFECT IN GULZAR'S WORDS

The central enquiry of this chapter is: how do Gulzar's words persuade us to resign from the position of a passive observer to become an active participant in a deeper, fuller experience of our existence, and invoke the caring custodian in us?

In this last section, a unique phenomenon is explored to admire the persuasiveness and authenticity of his reflections on soil and society. Named the 'Mona Lisa Effect,' it appears to be an ever-present quality of his work, which remains subterranean. Something like the third tributary of *Triveni*!

I have picked two *nazms* here to exemplify this phenomenon — to show how his words become a collective mirror in which an individual 'observer' can recognise their own humanity, hopes, despairs, and bondages.

Watch how his words actively draw us in and how we earnestly start partaking in Gulzar's despairs, ecstasy, compassion, or the urgency and responsibility that he experiences in these *nazms*:

> मैं अख़बार के पन्ने पर अपनी तस्वीर ढूंढता हूँ
> आज के दिन कितने मरे
> आज का स्कोर क्या है
> एहसास नहीं होता कि ज़िंदा हूँ
>
> कहाँ से ढूँढू मैं हाथ अपने
> कि मेरे हाथों पे और लोगों ने हाथ अपने चढ़ा दिए हैं
> अजीब है ये निज़ाम जिसमे,
> निज़ाम ने काट कर मेरे हाथ,
> कायदों और फ़ाईलों में छुपा दिए हैं (*Raat Pashmine Ki*, p 120)

The two *nazms* show how we, 'the observer', become 'the observed' — just like the known dynamism of Mona Lisa's enigmatic eyes that seem to follow and 'watch' the intrigued onlookers themselves.

Bringing a fresh understanding of the persuasiveness of his words on soil and society, I refer to it as the Mona Lisa Effect. It is hypothesised to be a result of the following qualities present in his work:

1) Only conscientious reflections of a fine and eternally present mind have the perceptiveness to 'watch' us with intimacy. Gulzar can pierce into the heart of the matter to un-layer the subtle, imperceptible, yet something universal. Because he is not opaque to himself, his reflections are piercing – collective:

मैं सिगरेट तो नहीं पीता...
मगर हर आने वाले से बस इतना पूछ लेता हूँ कि 'माचिस' है?"
बहुत कुछ है, जिसे मैं फूंक देना चाहता हूँ, मगर हिम्मत नहीं होती! (*Pluto*, p 105)

2) Whether it is a moment of beauty or poignancy, something magical-in-mundane or an elemental truth cocooned in a complex labyrinth of issues — Gulzar unveils the larger patterns and profound poetry of the moment with an amazing brevity. He can present the whole that is greater than the sum of its parts:

कितने मासूमों के घर दंगो में जल कर
मलबे का ढेर हुए जाते हैं गुजरात में...
...और ये है,
एक टूटे हुए रौज़न में इसे
तिनके सजाने की पड़ी है! (*Neglected Poem*, p 22)

सूरज की इस बैक-लाइट में घर के खंडहर ...
और दीवारों पर बैठे अफ़ग़ानी बच्चे,
अमेरिका के 'आर्ट जर्नल' के 'कवर पेज' पर
अब भी ज़िंदा लगते है!

हल्का हल्का धुआं निकलता रहता है! (*Pandrah Panch Pichattar*, p 37)

With these qualities, he brings in many layers of meaning and touchpoints so that a private reflection starts to eloquently speak to the collective. With these qualities, his words make the 'observer' recognise their own humanity and become the 'observed' — persuading us to turn inwards, away from pity and preaching, and towards perceptiveness!

Gulzar writes about the collective pain and jubilations only after perceiving it on an intimate and personal level. This is essential to becoming a custodian that actively cares for the welfare of our shared existence. As Osho said: "The more you become yourself, the more you will feel responsible for the world."

In our 2019 conversation, I asked the Moonsmith more questions about climate change and mankind's infringement into everything we should coexist with. His enlivening response is enclosed at the end of the book.

In closing this chapter, here is *nazm Padosi* a moving portrayal of how our lives are closely entwined with those we share our existence with:

जब तक मेरे सामने वाले घर में रौशनी जलती है
मेरे कमरे की दीवार पे
उस घर की परछाईआं चलती रहती हैं

कभी कभी यूँ भी होता है
उस घर के धुएं की परछाई, मेरी दीवार पे पड़ती है
तब लगता है।
दोनों घरों में आग लगी है! (*Suspected Poems*, Page 122)

GULZAR ON TIME... WAQT KI MAUJ

The hands of time point to 11:30. I enter his library when the Boskiyana sun is hiding behind him, and a misty, mystical aura fills the space. As I humbly stand in his sage-like aura for the very first time and touch his feet, my sense of time fades and the moment dissolves into the entirety of time!

That momentous morning with the Moonsmith in his library enabled me to experience time's paradox — I lost myself in its immeasurability and simultaneously amassed many grand moments.

That day we talk about what defines our experience of time and the ever-evolving nature of human existence — that time is incessant, yet it runs out; that it can be *pilpila,* yet often enslaving; that it is enriching to revisit bygone times, yet vital to perpetually renew us. That day we delight in the enduring nature of change — मैं जो पल पल बदलता रहता हूँ.

That day he shares the rare imagery of *pilpile lamhe* fresh out of his reverential diary — moments just like rubbery balls...

मैं अक्सर पिलपिले लम्हे उठा कर देखता रहता हूँ उंगली से दबाकर,
हर एक लम्हे मे कोई एक धड़कता हुआ वक़्त रखा है

As I 'orbited' the Moonsmith Gulzar extensively after that momentous 'landing' on Boskiyana, it became evident that the paradoxical nature of time enchants him. His words pay fertile awareness to the present and at once exhibit raw yearning for the bygone. He celebrates both the humanised concept of time and its celestial magnitude.

He can allot eternity to ephemeral moments and experience time in an unshackled manner — like a real time-lord! His words portray time's supremacy but without ever feeling enslaved in *kaal's* hand.

This chapter takes on the stunning and diverse allegories by the Moonsmith Gulzar on the concept of time that I captured while orbiting him.

वक़्त को आते न जाते न गुज़रते देखा
ना उतरते हुए देखा कभी इलहाम की सूरत
जमा होते हुए इक जगह मगर देखा है ... (*Selected Poems*, p 86)

In Gulzar's writings, time is both eternal and ephemeral. It is portrayed as both magnanimous and enslaving. It gets amassed in the form of days, months, and years, yet it remains elusive.

This chapter explores how has Gulzar duly honoured time's paradoxical dimensions through his diverse allegories on the concept of time — written with the tenderness of a poet, with the noble spirit of a philosopher, and some penned with worldly pragmatism.

KUCH BHI QAYAM NAHIN HAI — THE 'FLOW OF SHEER CHANGE'

Is it time that we experience, or simply 'the continuously flowing stream of sheer change?' (*Hannah Arendt,* 1981)

So then, is the term *time* just a grand tradition by mankind — only to assign significance to the brevity of our passage through the incessant stream of change? Reflecting on these, I wonder about how Gulzar has illuminated the many layers of these intriguing inquests on the dimension of time:

सच तो ये है कि ज़िंदगी जिस तरह से बहती है, और जिस तरह से बढ़ती है, चलती है, ये ज़िंदगी बिल्कुल ऐसी आज से बीस साल पहले नहीं थी, पचास साल पहले नहीं थी, एक सौ बरस पहले नहीं थी। तो ज़िंदगी एक कोई ठहरी हुई, कोई सिक्का बंद चीज़ तो है नहीं। It is something that keeps changing.

'Horizon keeps on extending further. That is the evolution of human beings,' he reminds me during our conversation in Boskiyana, quoting his nazm *Mustaqil*:

कुछ भी क़ायम नहीं है, कुछ भी नहीं

रात दिन गिर रहे हैं चौसर पर
औंधी सीधी सी कौडियों की तरह,
हाथ लगते हैं माह-ओ-साल मगर,
उंगलियों से फिसलते रहते हैं,
धूप छांव की दौड है सारी,
कुछ भी क़ायम नहीं है, कुछ भी नहीं

और जो क़ायम है, बस इक मैं हूँ
मैं जो पल पल बदलता रहता हूँ (*Pukhraj*, p 47)

In *Mustaqil,* he reinforces the 'continuously flowing stream of change' as the most enduring virtue of our existence. Juxtaposing this with *nazm Sabbath* draws out new layers of meaning. In *Sabbath,* Gulzar presents a poetic 'zoom out' to get the widest possible view of the kinship between the three: mankind, the incessant stream of change, and the experience of time in between:

आदमी बुलबुला है पानी का
और पानी की बहती सतह पर
टूटता भी है, डूबता भी है
फिर उभरता है, फिर से बहता है
ना समंदर निगल सका इसको

ना तवारीख़ तोड़ पायी है
वक़्त की मौज पर सदा बहता
आदमी बुलबुला है पानी का (*Pukhraj*, p 124)

Hinged on the exquisite allegory of '*Aadmi Bulbula Hai*,' this *nazm* is a rare poetic equation that elegantly positions mankind's transient timespan (*bulbula)* in relation to the eternally shifting waves of change (*waqt ki mauj)*.

In this equation, being bubble-like is the most defining dimension of human existence: ephemeral yet unwavering, insignificant yet triumphant — bound by the brevity of a certain timespan yet riding the perpetual wave of change.

A related poetic equation is depicted in this short *sketch* also:

ये वक़्त का थान खुलता रहता है पल-ब-पल
और लोग पोशाकें काटकर अपने अपने अंदाज़ से पहनते हैं वक़्त (*Pukhraj*, p 39)

Collectively *Sabbath* and *Mustaqil*, with anthem-like qualities, highlight the stunning paradox that the more we change and evolve, the more continuous and enduring the journey of mankind on the waves of *waqt* would be. 'Zooming into' the finer quality of humans to evolve enables us to 'zoom out' to the larger view of humankind's perpetuity.

I revisit the empowering imagery of these two *nazms* during the lockdown times amidst the global pandemic of COVID-19, pondering about what would make mankind buoyant, or bubble-like, on the waves of COVID-19 pandemic? What would resilience mean? Merely bouncing back to our old *adatein*, or being able to evolve significantly and swiftly to a new paradigm of living?

Sabbath brilliantly underlines that resilience constitutes the entire continuum of *tootna*, *doobna*, *phir se ubharna*, *phir se bahna* — not merely bouncing back to the original state. It acknowledges that mankind's ability to embrace this entire continuum of change is vital to our timelessness and tenacity:

> ...टूटता भी है, डूबता भी है
> फिर उभरता है, फिर से बहता है... (*Pukhraj*, p 124)

While discussing *Sabbath*, it is useful to note here how remarkably views of Gulzar, Rabindranath Tagore, Khalil Gibran, and Sarah Manguso converge on the kinship that *Sabbath* reflects:

> Gibran (1962): 'Man is like the foam of the sea that floats upon the surface of water...'

> Tagore (1913): 'Let your life lightly dance on the edges of time, like dew on the tips of a leaf.'

> Sarah Manguso (2015): 'The best thing about time passing is the privilege of running out of it, of watching the wave of mortality break over me and everyone I know ... Look at me, dancing my little dance for a few moments against the background of eternity.'

Gulzar's body of literary works with an enviable repertoire of fresh expressions and novel imagery is itself homage to 'continuously flowing stream of sheer change' and a testament to how to remain synchronous with time.

Like a cascading river, his work is enduring yet reflective of the sensitivities of changing times. It is deep, yet brimming with novelty and vitality, never stagnant.

This essence of his literary work is both to be marvelled at and vital to our literary heritage. This not only sets him apart from his contemporaries but also brilliantly exhibits how 'time' can be truly amassed by creating new and adapting to change.

Gulzar has categorically said no to ever becoming out-dated. He said, 'SMS और Facebook के ज़माने में डाकिया डाक लाया नही लिख सकता, ये मैं जानता हूँ' (*Hindustan Times*, 2014). In another interview, he remarked: 'Our poetry has to depict the reality of our times. Change is always for the better. I have learnt to adapt...' (*The Hindu*, 2008). He shares the same sentiments in the following *nazm*:

एक ज़माना कल गुज़रता था गली से
बड़ी रफ़्तार में था
ज़रा सा हट गया था मैं कि उसको रास्ता दे दूँ
मगर मुमकिन नहीं था
वो टकराया कहा
देखो रुकोगे तो गिरोगे
न जाने कब कलाई फँस गयी उसकी हज़ारों उँगलियों में
घिसटता, डगमगाता, उठता, गिरता चल रहा हूँ
मैं खुद से कह रहा हूँ अब
ज़माना चल रहा है, तुम रुकोगे तो गिरोगे
उफ़ दौड़-दौड़ के क़दम मिलाता हूँ
ये ज़िन्दगी कितनी तेज़ चलती है

Gulzar 'watches' everything vigilantly — the changing eras and generations, the pulse of evolving language, culture, and technology — just like *waqt*:

'वक़्त की आँख पर पट्टी नहीं बांधी जा सकती'

'THIS BLOODY TYRANT TIME'

जाने कैसे इस गर्दिश मे अटका पांव, धैय्या छूने से पहले ही —
वक़्त ने चोर कहा और आँखें खोल के
मुझको पकड लिया (*Raat Pashmine Ki*, p 12)

A tyrannical outlook of time and its enslaving effect on humanity is not absent from Gulzar's work. In such allegories, he presents time as a great leveller of life for all mankind, resonating with William J. Reilly (1945) that "everyone has the same amount to spend every day."

> मुझे खर्ची में पूरा एक दिन हर रोज़ मिलता है,
> मगर हर रोज़ कोई छीन लेता है, झपट लेता है अंटी से
>
> अभी दो चार लम्हे खर्च करने के लिये रख ले,
> बकाया उम्र के खाते मे लिख देते हैं, जब होगा हिसाब होगा (*Raat Pashmine Ki*, p 95)

I imagine that '*hisaab-kitaab*' and 'bartering,' whilst making delightful allegories of time, also subtly hint at its dominance, and invoke a sense of despair in the time-slaved cogs that we are.

The capitalistic timekeeping, the hardships of survival, or the slavery of our time-bound aspirations — some of his contemplations on harsh realities of time are shared here:

> वक़्त बैठा हुआ है गर्दन पर, तोड़ता जा रहा है टुकड़ों मे
> ज़िंदगी दे के भी नहीं चुकते,
> ज़िंदगी के जो कर्ज़ देने हों (*Pukhraj*, p 97)
>
> गुलाम है वक़्त गर्दिशों का,
> कि जैसे उसका ग़ुलाम हूँ मैं (*Raat Pashmine Ki*, p 14)
>
> उम्मीद बड़ी ही चिकनी डली है
> ऊपर से बरसता है वक़्त, पल को रुकता नही (*Pluto*, p 108)
>
> हाथ लगते हैं माह-ओ-साल मगर,
> उंगलियों से फिसलते रहते हैं

Our attempts to hold on to the elusive time and to account for the 'flowing stream of change' in measurable units can sometimes be enslaving because it fuels our futile obsession with productivity and permanence. In contrast, calm acceptance of the transient nature of *waqt* can bring a lush presence to how alive we are and vastness to our soul.

The next section discusses the potent allegory of *Pilpile Lamhe* by the Moonsmith, presenting a contrast to the enslaving dimensions of time.

PILPILE LAMHE

A breathtaking allegory, *Pilpile Lamhe* is the quality to be eternally and passionately present in the heart of moments whilst being fully aware of the ever-transient nature of time.

This is how Gulzar describes it as I amass countless *pilpile lamhe* in his magical aura in *Boskiyana*:

> A moment is not a sheer moment. A moment has entire time caught into it. And: A moment gives birth to another moment and another — they are all pregnant. And they are pregnant not only with moments but with the entire time.

मैं अक्सर पिलपिले लम्हे उठा कर देखता रहता हूँ उंगली से दबाकर,
हर एक लम्हे मे कोई एक धड़कता हुआ वक़्त रखा है
...बड़े ज़र्खेज़* होते हैं ये लम्हे
कोई तो हामला होते हैं और उनसे और लम्हे जन्म लेते हैं

*ज़र्खेज़ — fecund, fertile

In the luminous *Boskiyana*-sun, as he recites this '*kachchi' nazm* fresh out of his reverential diary, time becomes non-existent — as though I am watching a deeply moving cosmic event with passionate presence. Indeed, the fecund, fertile moments that I collect in his company that morning will continue to germinate countless new panoramas and perspectives in me for years to come.

How to access *pilpile lamhe*? To this, he says:

> नब्ज़ पे हाथ रख कर देखिये वक़्त की — कि अब धड़कता है कि नहीं धड़कता? जब तक वो ज़िंदा है वो धड़कता है। Keep your antennas open. क्योंकि कोई लम्हा नहीं है जो ज़िंदगी आपको छूके ना गुज़रती हो। It is up to you how many of them can you capture.

His instantly empowering words remind me of the *nazm* '*dhoop ka purza*', where a routine moment — with Gulzar's unedited and 'real-time' attention and with all his senses poetically vigilant — turns into a vibrant, *pilpila* moment:

> शाम का सूरज जाते जाते
> दरवाजे के नीचे से
> धूप का इक छोटा सा पुरज़ा फेंक गया है (*Neglected Poems*, p 38)

This generous and non-discriminatory experience of moments can also be named love... and in *nazm Khuda* below, he speaks about such *lamhe* containing the elixir of life to counter the *Kaal,* to become 'time-lords' in the real sense:

> काल चला तुमने और मेरी जानिब देखा,
> मैने काल को तोड़ कर लम्हा-लम्हा जीना सीख लिया
>
> पूरे का पूरा आकाश घुमा कर अब तुम देखो बाज़ी (*Yaar Julahe*, p 61)

But in Gulzar's work, the power of *pilpile lamhe* is not complete without recognising the power of the past or the *maazi* — because 'a moment has entire time caught into it'.

> क्योंकि आपका past आपके साथ है, तो आपको उसी मे से germinate करके एक नया rhythm पैदा करना पड़ता है...

The past is never absent! The generative virtues of the past lend a rare potency and poignancy to the present moments making them truly *pilpile* with the layers and blood and flesh and bones of time. But the true power of the past is that it lends a cyclic nature to the experience of time, as conveyed in the *nazm Umr*:

...लेकिन उम्र का ये सफ़र दो तरफ़ा है
जैसे जैसे आगे बढ़ती जाती है उम्र
पीछे की तस्वीरें सामने आने लगती है
कई बार जी चाहता है कि अपने माज़ी से जाकर फिर से मिला जाये
या, अपने माज़ी को सामने ले ले, इसके साथ साथ चले

This making sense of the future via the past is another essence of *pilpile lamhe*. Revisiting the past — not to indwell in nostalgia but only for wilful travel back in time to enrich the present — is something Gulzar is fascinated with. He shares this in an interview:

अतीत मेरे लिये हमेशा ही बहुत रहस्यमय रहा है … अतीत शायद सभी को मोहित करता है — फॅसिनेट करता है। अतीत को देखने और छूने की इच्छा हर साधारण आदमी मे रहती है। उम्र के साथ साथ आदमी बहुत दूर-दूर तक निकल जाता है और फिर उन वक़्तों को ढूंढता, देखता और छूने की कोशिश करता है।

To capture such longing to re-touch the pulse of bygone times, he created the vigorous allegory of '*Hamila hoon yaad se*' (carrying a memory) or the near-universal nostalgia in '*Dil Dhoondta hai,*' where he masterfully turns long-gone mundane moments into precious *pilpile lamhe*.

"If nostalgia could itself write, it would write like you," I cannot resist saying this to my Moonsmith that day!

Here are these two *nazms* exhibiting how bygone times enrich our present:

मैं अब भी हामिला हूँ याद से उसकी
वो लड़की अब भी मुझे याद आती है (*Raat Pashmine Ki*, p 104)

या गर्मियों की रात जब पुरवाइयां चलें
ठंडी सफेद चादरों पे जागें देर तक
तारों को देखते रहें छत पर पड़े हुए (*Pukhraj*, p 102)

In closing this chapter, here is *nazm Mausam* that poignantly brings together the many perspectives of time discussed in this chapter.

Mausam is a sensing portrayal of changing seasons where the Moonsmith unveils an eternal truth about time: that the generative markings of the bygone season will be detectible in the fertility and fecundity of forthcoming harvests. Reminding that how we look back is how we look forward. As Paulo Coelho says in *The Zahir* (2005): "Past contains the answers to the future."

ग़ौर से देखना बहारों में
पिछले मौसम के भी निशां होंगे
कोंपलों की उदास आँखों में
आंसुओं की नमी बची होगी (*Pukhraj*, p 64)

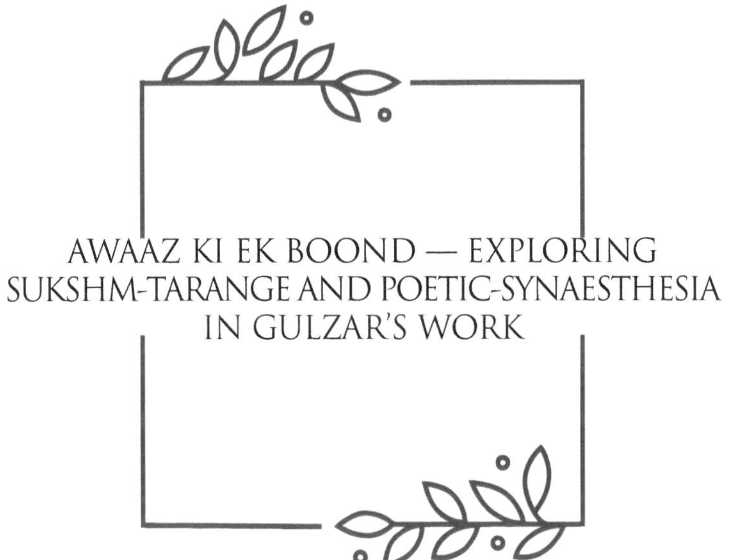

AWAAZ KI EK BOOND — EXPLORING SUKSHM-TARANGE AND POETIC-SYNAESTHESIA IN GULZAR'S WORK

I said to the Moonsmith once that this chapter takes on the concept of synaesthesia to explore the rare and elegant commingling of senses in his poetry. Someone with Synaesthesia may be able to 'hear' colours or 'see' voices. I say to him that research suggests that we all might be Synaesthesia in infancy. He smiles, sharing that he still preserves the child in him...remains childlike!

Humne dekhi hai un ankhon ki mahakti khushboo marks a momentous time when a spectacular crossing of the senses started to imbue his words and emerged as one of the most delineating qualities of his work — single-handedly and almost overnight, bringing a beautiful disruption to the prosaic!

In an interview, he shared how some found it objectionable that he attributed a sense of smell to the eyes. He says, "...for me, just as there's no definition of a poet, there's no definition of poetry."

Breaking the conventional structure of poetry, experimentation with poetic-grammar, and not typecasting the five senses! How does he remain unshackled from these bondages? This is how he describes a similar experience to me in Boskiyana: ये जिस्म मुझसे अलग भी है, मेरे साथ भी है...

> ...मैं जब ख़लाओं के अरज़े मे घूमने निकलता हूँ...
> किसी भी राह के पत्थर पे बैठा देखता है
> मैं इसकी ग्रॅविटी से कैसे खोल कर गिरहें अकेला क़ायनात मे घूमता हूँ...

How do we unshackle from gravity? How do we become empty? Childlike? How do we grow to be unselfconscious and forsake our loved overgrown jungle of knowledge, beliefs, and habits?

This chapter curiously deals with the presence of *sukshm-tarange* and poetic-synaesthesia in Gulzar's work that can only flow from a 'blank-point' of nothingness — only after emptying any pre-conditioning of what the mind is meant to mind, and the senses meant to sense!

वो जो शायर था, चुप-सा रहता था
बहकी-बहकी-सी बातें करता था
आँखें कानों पे रखके सुनता था
गूंगी ख़ामोशियों की आवाज़ें (*Pukhraj*, p 31)

Gulzar can transcend the fragmented physicalities of the conventional five senses. Touching the limitlessness of the moment, he can write that which cannot be seen, heard, or touched.

This chapter explores the concept of *sukshm-tarange* and Synaesthesia in Gulzar's work as being quintessential to how he creates '*bhawnaon ki tarlata*.' It is like witnessing the act of an illusionist!

Sukshm-tarange is discussed as the quality of touching the tender intersection of conscious and subconscious:

दिमाग़ की गीली-गीली सोचों से
भीगी-भीगी उदास यादें टपक रही हैं

Poetic-synaesthesia is discussed as the quality of mixing multiple senses:

सांस लेती हुई आँखें अक्सर बोलती रहती हैं गूंगी बातें

Both *sukhsm-tarange* and poetic-synaesthesia are manifestations of a fine mind that has touched the deepest and subtlest levels of consciousness. Both expressions are incredibly rare, yet desirable, to attain poetic fluidity and transcendence.

SUKSHM-TARANGE IN GULZAR'S WORK

John Cage said: 'Music brings the conscious and subconscious together by providing a moment when, awareness of time and space being lost, the multiplicity of elements which make up an individual become integrated and he is one.'

These lines flow just like this, like music — with imagery so subliminal and supernal that seems virtually impossible to create with free will:

> रूह देखी है कभी रूह को महसूस किया है?
> जागते-जीते हुए दूधिया कोहरे से लिपटकर
> सांस लेते हुए इस कोहरे को महसूस किया है? (*Pukhraj*, p 71)

Only by shedding past influences, unlearning the learnt, and by holding on to it 'till you get exactly what you have felt', can one begin to access the subtle, tender intersection of the brain and soul. Only by beginning from a point of nothing, can the moment encompass everything.

There are countless instances of this state of self-transcendence in Gulzar's work, where the 'I' dissolves into complete surrender — granting a great gradient for his words to flow from conscious to subconscious. This is how he — in Seasmus Heaney's words — "makes possible a fluid and the restorative relationship between the mind's centre and its circumference." Consider the fluidity in the following lines that is truly instinctive, intuitive, and involuntary:

> कितनी आवाज़ें हैं, ये लोग हैं, बातें हैं मगर
> ज़हन के पीछे किसी और ही सतह पे कहीं
> जैसे चुपचाप बरसता है तसव्वुर तेरा (*Pukhraj*, p 17)

Was Amrita Pritam perhaps referring to this quality when she wrote that 'Gulzar is finely tuned to *sukshm-tarange?*' Another fine example of *sukshm-tarange* and self-transcendence is presented in the *nazm* Mariam. It is testimony to how he writes sub-sensations that cannot be perceived with conventional senses:

रात में देखो झील का चेहरा
किस क़दर पाक, पुरसुकूँ, ग़मगीं
कोई साया नहीं है पानी पर
कोई सिलवट नहीं हैं आँखों में
नींद आ जाये दर्द को जैसे
जैसे मरियम उदास बैठी हो
जैसे चेहरा हटाके चेहरे का
सिर्फ एहसास रख दिया हो वहाँ (*Pukhraj*, p 94)

More examples are presented below where Gulzar transcends beyond what ordinary minds can see, feel, touch, hear and sense — to the subtlest, to the *sukshm-tarange*:

तुमने सोचा तो होगा - देखा नहीं
ख़ुश्क सहरा पे जब बरस जाये
एक छलका हुआ, भरा सावन
देर तक रेत सरसराती है (*Pukhraj*, p 44)

आँखों और कानो में कुछ सन्नाटे-से भर जाते हैं
क्या तुमने उड़ती देखी है, रेत कभी तन्हाई की (*Yaar Julahe*, p 139)

सभी धुंधला गया फिर से
अँधेरा फिर से बहने लग गया है
पिघलकर फिर कोई शै बह रही है (*Pluto*, p 35)

तेरी नज़्म से गुज़रते वक़्त, ख़दशा रहता है
पाँव रख रहा हूँ जैसे

गीले लैंडस्केप पर, इमरोज़ के! (*Pluto*, p 78)

दिल में ऐसे ठहर गए हैं ग़म
जैसे जंगल में शाम के साये (*Pukhraj*, p 116)

और हवाओं में भी सूराख़ पड़े हैं

और वक़्त भी बासी था जब आया था शहर में
हर शाख़ से लिपटे हुए सन्नाटे खड़े थे (*Pukhraj*, p 66)

These poems are manifestations of an exceptionally fine mind that can touch the undetectable vibrations of the universe, without a bias to the bliss or the melancholy in it. Basu Bhattacharya's observation holds a vital clue to Gulzar's rare ability for such poetic subtlety:

> मुझे गुलज़ार के मस्तिष्क के कुहरे की जानकारी है, जिसमे ना तो रात का अंधकार है, ना दिन का बिल्कुल सॉफ उजाला ही — वो तो उस भोर या सांझ की तरह है, जिसका प्रकाश इतना कोमल होता है कि वह अपने पीछे कोई परछाई नहीं छोड़ पाती और अंधकार इतना धीमा होता है कि वह कोई चीज़ छुपा भी नहीं पाती। (*Gulzar ek Shakshiyat*, p 42)

Gulzar does not typecast experiences. And he does not typecast senses, he unifies them. The crossing of the senses is another awe-inspiring aspect of his works and is discussed as poetic-synaesthesia in the next section.

POETIC-SYNAESTHESIA IN GULZAR'S WORK

Can eyes be fragrant, and can fragrance be seen? हमने देखी हैं उन आँखों की महकती ख़ुशबू...

Can a voice touch us in the flesh and blood, can it be touched or pinned to an album?

इक अनजान आवाज़ ने छूकर पूछा था... (*Pukhraj*, p 22)

Can the touch of hands be heard? तुम्हारे हाथ क्यों इस क़दर ख़ामोश रहते हैं?...

Such a spectacular union of senses is one of the most delineating qualities of Gulzar's work. Without aiming to demystify this phenomenon, the rare and fascinating neurological state called Synaesthesia — or crossing of the senses — is adopted here only as a curious framework to gain insight into the workings of a mind that can transcend beyond the limitations of isolated five senses.

In Synaesthesia, the stimulation of one sensory pathway leads to involuntary experiences in a second sensory pathway. This may cause sounds to have a peculiar colour (for example *santoor* notes wear a bright yellow sound), days to have their own *mehak*, or a voice to have a peculiar touch!

> तेरे उतारे हुए दिन पहन के अब भी मैं
> तेरी महक में कई रोज़ काट देता हूँ!! (*Neglected Poem*, p 44)

Indeed, according to writers Simon Baron-Cohen and John E. Harrison, 'We might all be colour-hearing Synesthetes until we lose connections between these two areas somewhere about three months of age when clear distinction and segregation of senses occurs.'

Just like a Synesthete's experience of less segregation and more harmony with the universe's fluidity and infiniteness, we can also experience — through Gulzar's unique creative outpouring — a kaleidoscope of sensations fused into each other.

He creates a mind-bending, infinite playground for the senses where the resonant, sonorous voice touches us like misty drizzle (*bauchhar*), and smouldering eyes can feel icy-cold. Consider these examples where we are initiated to this fluid world of fused senses:

> तेरी आवाज़ की बौछार में भीगा नहीं हूँ मैं (*Raat Pashmine Ki*, p 57)

पीछे पीछे आती तेरी दो आँखों की चाप सुनायी देती है (*Raat Pashmine Ki*, p 125)

तन पे लगती हैं चिपकती आँखें
बर्फ सी ठंडी, सुलगती आँखें (*Pukhraj*, p 129)

मेज़ कुर्सी है कि ख़ामोशी के धब्बे जैसे (*Pukhraj*, p 118)

तेरी आवाज़ की एक बूँद जो मिल जाए कहीं (*Pukhraj*, p 118)

तुम्हारे हाथ क्यों इस क़दर खामोश रहते हैं (*Pluto*, p 30)

कान पर धीमे से रख दूंगा आवाज़ के दो होंट (*Pukhraj*, p 126)

वरना उधड़ी उधड़ी नींदें ओढ़ के दोनों,
फीके सपने चाट चाटके, रात गुज़ारा करती है! (*Pluto*, p 32)

आँखों को भी इक चुप-सी लग जाती है
उँगलियों से छूता हूँ तेरी ख़ामोशी तब
'ब्रेल' में लिखी तेरी बातें पढता हूँ!! (*Pluto*, p 24)

तेरी आवाज़ को कागज़ पे रख के, मैंने चाहा था
कि पिन कर लूँ (*Raat Pashmine Ki*, p 57)

मैंने मुन्द्रों की तरह कानों में
तेरी आवाज़ पहन रक्खी है (*Pukhraj*, p 21)

खुशबू के रंग हैं तो बता
मेहंदी पहनू या महुवा [*Maula* (One Above)]

All colours deserve a 'hearing' and all sounds deserve a 'touch'! In these selected excerpts, Gulzar grants them exactly that — by exhibiting a rare 'palette' of senses that is beyond any discrimination, or any cultural and social pre-conditioning of what the senses are meant to sense.

Alan Watt in his lecture *The Unspeakable World* said, "All

these things, without being named, and saying 'that is a shadow, that is red, that is brown, that is somebody's foot'...when you don't name things any longer, you start seeing them..."

Watts goes on to say, "The world of color is infinite, as is the world of sound. And it is only through stopping fixing conceptions on the world of color and sound that you really begin to hear it and see it." For support, he quotes this poem of Lao-Tzu:

The five colours blind the eye.
The five tones deafen the ear.
The five flavours dull the taste.
Racing and hunting madden the mind.
Precious things lead one astray.

Therefore, the sage is guided by what
he feels and not by what he sees.
He lets go of that and chooses this.

Gulzar chooses this! He chooses a world of infinite colours and sounds to truly see and hear what he is feeling... without, as Alan Watt says, "The [mental] chatter!"

These virtues of *sukshm-tarange* and poetic-synaesthesia truly set him apart from his contemporaries.

In concluding this chapter, here is *Raat Taameer Karein,* where, by 'touching' and commingling various sensations, Gulzar 'paints' the ultimate etherealness of a moment from the womb of infinity:

एक रात चलो तामीर करें
ख़ामोशी के संगे -मरमर पर,
हम तान के तारीकी सर पर,
दो शम्माएं जलाये जिस्मों की!
जब ओस दबे पांव उतरे,
आहट भी न पाये साँसों की,

कोहरे की रेशमी ख़ुशबू में,
ख़ुशबू की तरह ही लिपटे रहे।

और जिस्म के सोंधे पर्दों में,
रूहों की तरह लहराते रहे!! (*Raat Pashmine Ki*, p 76)

Nazmon Ke Taanke — Gulzar's Insights on the Creative Process

It has taken me over six, some full and some part, years to write and rewrite the nine chapters of this book...

During this time, my Moonsmith would sometimes read portions of my writings and convey his feedback despite a million things competing for his attention. One remarkably transformative moment occurred in 2016 when, with dreams in eyes and the manuscript in hands, I had visited him in Boskiyana.

It was the day when my 'orbit path' was to change greatly as he told me in unambiguous words that the manuscript needed more '*pakna*', more ripening. He encouraged me to go beyond my comfort boundaries, advising me to 'write original thoughts and articles' before compiling a book.

The 'breaking' that occurred within me that day was restored by the gold of his guidance. Just like the Ancient Japanese Art of Kinsugi for fixing broken pottery or golden repair, I felt precious, one-of-a-kind, with my unique fault-lines shining in pure 'white' gold...

Every time I presented my creative curiosities to him, he would patiently answer them and always remind me to learn about life, read extensively, and then read some more. He would also remind me not to love our overgrown jungle of knowledge, beliefs, and other influences.

What propels creativity? What may be involved in nourishing literature, and how to dissolve our influences while still making personal possessions through our creativity?

As I orbited the Moonsmith Gulzar, four distinct areas of his creative process were captured:

- मरने के बाद ही करता हूँ मैं हर नज़्म हमेशा...
- अपने पहचान की तस्वीरें लिए जाता है...
- ये सब मंझेंगी...
- दुकान पे रोज़ बैठता हूँ...

This chapter curiously orbits these terrains to get a rare glimpse into his creative impetus and practices.

खुलने लगे हैं आसमान की सिरे उफ़क़ से
कितनी जगह से अब ये ख़ैमा उधड़ रहा है
सारा दिन बैठा नज़्मों के टाँके लगा कर
उस को रफ़ू करता हूँ! (*Green Poems*, p 74)

Much has been written on the golden rules of creativity and its many touchstones. Yet, few match the eloquence and brevity of Gulzar's creative manifesto in *jagah nahin diary me*.

Fluid but crisp, this nazm is as much about surrendering to inner calling as it is about having a sustained act of will — a complete manifesto of what the process of creativity encapsulates. An excerpt is presented here.

...कुछ ऐसी नज़्में जो तोड़ कर फेंक दी थीं उसमें
धुआँ न निकले
कुछ ऐसे अश'आर जो मिरे 'ब्रांड' के नहीं थे
वो एक ही कश में खांसकर, ऐश ट्रे में
घिस के बुझा दिए थे...
इस ऐशट्रे में,
'ब्लेड' से काटी रात की नब्ज़ से टपकते
सियाह क़तरे बुझे हुए हैं...
छिले हुए चाँद की त्राशें,
जो रात भर छील-छील कर फेंकता रहा हूँ... (*Neglected Poems*, p 110)

This chapter attempts to get a glimpse into the creative impetus and practices that Gulzar has often alluded to.

The aim is not to demystify the ineffable creative modus operandi of a master craftsman, but to explore the four distinct and important areas of the creative process that he has often reflected upon in his written or spoken words:

1) Dissolving the influences
2) Making possible the deepest kind of personal possession of the world
3) The incubation period in creativity
4) Importance of a steady writing regime

DISSOLVING THE INFLUENCES

मरने के बाद ही करता हूँ मैं हर नज़्म हमेशा...

Gulzar has often voiced his deep connection with literature and its genesis being a very lonely process. "To create literature, you have to live in a cave ... and that cave is nothing but you," he said during his Sydney visit in January 2018.

Relishing his coffee at The Rocks, in the suburb of Sydney, he was referring to that state of self-transcendence when we throw ourselves out of us and carve out our own 'cave.' This dissolving of influences is particularly relevant in this era when soot of information continues to settle on our minds. Not to mention our unprecedented fetish for self-importance and possessiveness of our assimilated knowledge. This 'dissolving of influences' is what he speaks of in the following nazms:

मरने से पहले कोई नज़्म नहीं होती कभी दोस्त
मरने के बाद ही करता हूँ मैं हर नज़्म हमेशा (*Pluto*, p 81)

जो मैं अपनी उम्र उधेड़ के, साँसें तोड़ के देता हूँ
नज़्में क्यों नाराज होती हैं?

वो सारी नज़्में, कि मैं समझता हूँ वह मेरे
'जीन ' से हैं लेकिन
तो यूँ समझती हैं उन से है मेरा नाक नक्शा
शक्ल उन से मिली है मुझ को

To become a 'cave' by transcending the overgrown jungle of knowledge and influences is one of the biggest challenges every artist faces. Gulzar offers an antidote: To persist! 'Hold-on till you get exactly what you have felt!' Hold on until one finds the most chaste and honest expression to articulate the emotion, moment, or memory. This indefatigability of disentangling the influences, according to Gulzar, is indispensable for creating something original. In an interview he elaborated on this:

> वो लिखें जो महसूस करते हैं. किताबों के हवालों से inspire, influence होंगे तो वो तो change होता जायेगा, वो लिखें जो आप खुद महसूस करते हैं। So, hold on, do not just get rid of it. अगर छोड़ देंगे तो वो आम हो जायेगा but hold on to it till you get exactly what you have felt. Then it will be different that will be yours, that will be a novelty. Originality comes from there. उसको संभालना, बर्दाश्त करना और ईमानदार रहना — वो सब उसमे शामिल है।

The following two *nazms* from his poetry collection Pluto instantly became my favourite. Only to understand later that these are a testament to how he conscientiously 'holds-on' to the veracity of the experience 'till he gets exactly what he has felt'— rather than assigning merit to the restraints of rhyming or rigidity of any format. He says in an interview: "The meaning and thought behind a poem are more important than the need to justify a rhyme." (*Jiya Jale,* p55)

"उस से कहना..."
इतना कहा ... और गर्दन नीची कर के
देर तलक वो पैर के अंगूठे से मिटटी खोद-खोदके
बात का बीज था, शायद, ढूंढ रही थी
देर तलक ख़ामोश रही ...
नाक से सिसकी पोंछ के आख़िर
गर्दन को कन्धे पे डाल के बोली,
"बस...इतना कह देना!" (*Pluto*, p 25)

उस दिन की तो बात है, मेरा छोटा बेटा
पिछले किसी बरस की दीवाली का छोटा..
एक अनार उठा लाया था!
बेमौका, बेमौसम, जब वो जल रहा था,
कितना सूना लगा था आँगन!
कितने बरसों बाद तुम्हारा बेमौसम इक खत पहुँचा है! (*Pluto*, p 43)

A hallmark of Gulzar's work — this quality of conscientiousness (दयानतदारी) is the virtue of experiencing a moment with singular honesty and diligence and then expressing it with such exactitude that it carries life, beauty, and truth of universal resonance. Consider these *nazms*:

इतना ऊंचा-ऊंचा बोलते हैं दो झरने आपस में
जैसे एक देहात के दोस्त अचानक मिल कर वादी में
गांव भर का पूछते हों (*Neglected Poems*, 64)

गोल फूला हुआ सूरज का गुब्बारा थककर
एक नोकीली पहाड़ी पे यूँ जाके टीका है
जैसे ऊँगली पे मदारी ने उठा रक्खा है गोला

फुँक से ठेलो तो पानी में उतर जायेगा नीचे
भक से फट जायेगा फुला हुआ सूरज का गुब्बारा
छन से बुझ जायेगा इक और दहकता हुआ दिन (*Pukhraj*, p161)

The ability to be conscientious is not only vital to imbuing novelty in creative expressions but possibly the only pathway to gain true freedom as a writer. To shed influences, carve out a 'cave' — and reach the ultimate truth!

Bhushan Vanmali wrote this about Gulzar's ability for self-transcendence: शायरी अपने शायर को तंग पिंजरे में क़ैद कर लेती है मगर बड़ी शायरी अपने शायर को अस्तित्व के बड़े पिंजरे में आज़ाद कर देती है — गुलज़ार आज़ाद हो गया।

MAKING POSSIBLE THE 'DEEPEST KIND OF PERSONAL POSSESSION OF THE WORLD'

अपने पहचान की तस्वीरें लिए जाता है...

During his Sydney visit, Gulzar shared another important insight into the genesis of literature: 'People ask me why I don't write autobiographical accounts?' After a brief pause, he added: 'The entire body of a writer's work is autobiographical — what can be more autobiographical than that?' I am reminded of the following *nazm.*

मैं नज़्में ओढ़ कर बैठा हुआ हूँ,
ठिठुरने लगता हूँ
कोना उठता है कोई जब कहीं से,
किसी मिसरे के अंदर झाँक कर छूता है कोई,
मेरे नंगे बदन पर कंपकपी दौड़ जाती है,

बिना नज़्मों के नंगा हूँ मै अंदर से,
बहोत सी चोटें तस्वीरों के अंदर ढाँप रखी है

From the beginning of time, writers have accessed their inner world of pains, sufferings, joys, struggles, hopes, or hurtful segments of their past as inputs into their creative process. What can be more intimate and personal than this? कवि का परिचय उसकी कविताएं ही हैं — वही उसकी दुनिया है, उसकी ज़िंदगी है,

इसका सफ़र है, संघर्ष है, कविताओं से ज्यादा व्यक्तिगत कुछ नहीं, he said in an interview.

Indeed, writers' words make them belong to the world and make the world belong to them! Their poems are an intimate invitation to hold their hands and go on a pilgrimage to every recess, every crevice of their mind and soul:

थक जाओ अगर —
और तुमको ज़रुरत पड़ जाए,
इक नज़्म की ऊँगली थाम के वापस आ जाना!

"Poetry makes possible the deepest kind of personal possession of the world..." — in the lines below Gulzar alludes to this vital and elevating role of an artist:

जिस तरह छोटी सी इस गर्म ज़मीं पर
बेपनाह ज़िंदा व बेजान ख़लाओं से गुज़रता शायर
अपनी पहचान की तसवीरें इकट्ठी किए जाता है
लिखे जाता है (*Pukhraj*, p 56)

बूँद से लेकर पूरे समन्दर तक
कहीं भी रुकता है पानी तो,
आँख खुली रहती है उसकी
सारे अक्स उतारता है!

पानी की इक बूँद है शायर
पूरा समन्दर अपनी आंख में रखता है!! (*Pluto*, p 73)

In *Boskiyana*, in response to my nervousness about bringing my vantage points to his words, he speaks to the process of making personal possessions via creativity:

> But you can! अगर Shakespere ने या ग़ालिब ने जो लिखा था, उसका वही मतलब होता जो वो कह रहा है, तो उसके re-interpretation की क्या ज़रुरत थी? The only thing is: उसमे layers

> हैं! उसने जिस ज़िन्दगी के बारे में कहा है, वो ज़िन्दगी बदल गयी वक़्त के साथ — and yet if it is the truth — वो फिर पैदा होगी, वो फिर उसमे जगह ढूंढ लेगा ... और वो बदलता रहेगा —इसलिए re-interpretation होती रहेगी, होती रहेगी, जिसको वो जिस point-of-view से नज़र आ जाए।
>
> एक ही sunset — मैंने describe किया, but fivc thousand people on the beach will see the same sunset differently. You have said this also. Everybody has the liberty to reinterpret it as they conceive it reveals to us — that it applies to my life like this.

This reads like a beautiful prelude to James Dickey's (1985) sagacious lines, "The sun of poetry is new every day, too, because it is seen in different ways by different people who have lived under it, lived with it, responded to it... Poetry makes possible the deepest kind of personal possession of the world..." In *Boskiyana*, Gulzar also delves into the nut and bolts of making such personal possessions:

> सारा कुछ ख़ुद आप-बीती नहीं होती। लेकिन आपकी जो observation है, किसी भूखे को देख कर जो महसूस किया मैने – that becomes my आपबीती। वो एहसास जो मेरे अन्दर उतरा है उसे देख के, वो मेरा हिस्सा बन गया है। वो सिर्फ बाहर नहीं रह गया। तो आप ज़िंदगी तो चारों तरफ देखते हैं। इसलिये आप हर बात पर लिख भी नहीं सकते। कहीं ना कहीं आप की observation है कहीं ना कहीं आप का experience है। लेकिन आप शामिल ज़रूर हैं उस creativity मे जो आपने लिखा है।

What about our *Aap-Beeti* and the trials and tribulations of our own life? How do they nourish the creative process? Gulzar's work on two powerful transformative forces is explored here to examine this: How he assuages confronting past and pain through his creative process.

ASSUAGING CONFRONTING PAST AND SUBLIMATING PAIN

During our Sydney conversation, listening intently to my questions 'Can becoming a creative medium unburden pain?' and 'has *Two*, his new novel, been able to sublimate the deep-seated pain of the Partition?,' he had admitted without delay: 'That's why I wrote it.'

The Partition of India has indeed been a defining element of Gulzar's works. The pain and imagery of the event became the soul of some of his iconic *nazms*, and a centrepiece of his theatre and some cinematic works also. *Dina* is a beloved muse and a subject of emotional excess for him. In his own words:

> विभाजन मेरी लेखनी का बहुत अहम हिस्सा है क्योंकि बहुत शुरुआती ज़िंदगी में वो दौर देखा और उसका असर आज तक है ... आज भी कहीं सांप्रदायिक दंगे देखता हूं, तो मुझे विभाजन की ही याद आती है और उससे तक़लीफ़ होती है।
>
> A part of me was left behind in Pakistan. My trauma is the trauma of that place. I am searching for that lost half. वो वतन था, ये देश है।

Like the incense that gives fragrance as it smoulders, *nazm Dastak* is a testament that confronting a hurtful past and searching for the 'lost half' can give birth to potent, healing imagery:

> सुबह सुबह इक ख़्वाब की दस्तक पर दरवाज़ा खोला, देखा
> सरहद के उस पार से कुछ मेहमान आये हैं...
> ख़्वाब था शायद ख़्वाब ही होगा
> सरहद पर कल रात, सुना है, चली थी गोली
> सरहद पर कल रात, सुना है
> कुछ ख़्वाबों का ख़ून हुआ था (*Yaar Julahe*, p 93)

Here are some of his iconic *nazms* pulsating with his signature poignancy about the lost *watan*, *galiyan*, *aangan*, *ghar*, *chulhe*:

कश्मीर से आये हुए पंडित
अपने नाम पर घरों को ख़त लिखतें हैं
ताकि मेरे छूटे हुए घर में
कोई आता जाता तो रहेगा (*India New England News*, 2015)

वतन अब भी वही है, पर नहीं है मुल्क अब मेरा
वहां जाना हो अब तो दो-दो सरकारों के
दसीयों दफ़्तरों से
शक्ल पर लगवा के मोहरे ख़्वाब साबित
करने पड़ते हैंI (*Raat Pashmine Ki*, p 60)

न जाने कौनसी मट्टी वतन की मट्टी थी
नज़र में धूल, जिगर में लिए ग़ुबार चले
ये फ़ासले तेरी गलियों के हमसे तय न हुए
हज़ार बार रुके हम, हज़ार बार चले
ये कैसी सरहदें उलझी हुई हैं पैरों में
हम अपने घर की तरफ मुड़ के बार बार चले (*Mammo*, 1994 Film)

अभी कुछ और भी दिल हैं
कि जिन को बांटने का, काटने का काम जारी है
वो बटवारा तो पहला था
अभी कुछ और बटवारे भी, बाक़ी हैं!! (*Raat Pashmine Ki*, p 99)

वतना वे, ओ मेरियाँ वतना वे
बट गए तेरे आँगन
बुझ गए चूल्हे सांझे
लुट गयी तेरी हीरें
मर गए तेरे रांझे
कौन तुझे पानी पूछेगा, फसलें सींचेगा
कौन तेरी माटी में ठन्डी छाँव बीजेगा
बैरी काट के ले गए तेरियां ठंडियां छावां वे
हम न रहे तो कौन बसाएगा तेरा वीराना

मुड़ के हम न देखेंगे और तू भी याद न आना
गिट्टे कन्चे बाँट के,
कर ली कुट्टी वतना वे
वतना वे! (*Pinjar*, 2003 Film)

To be able to articulate confronting past events is not only a privilege of writers but also a responsibility, for their words reach the hearts and souls of many, carrying seeds of transformation and healing. *Footprints on Zero Line* is a brilliant anthology of his writings on the Partition.

Fulfilling another vital responsibility of literature, Gulzar has also duly dignified the deep kinship of the anguishes of the heart and creative outpour! In *Boskiyana*, we delve deeper into the anatomy of *dard* when I ask him," दर्द आपकी हर writing मे बहुत positive connotation के साथ होता है। क्या ज़िंदगी मे दर्द अच्छे होते हैं, क्या एक कशिश है उसमे? His response makes my heart sing:

> आपने मोहब्बत की है ना? तो मोहब्बत जैसी खूबसूरत चीज़ मे भी दर्द तो है ना, उसके बग़ैर वो ख़ूबसूरत भी नहीं है। अगर उसमे दर्द ही ना होता तो कोई मोहब्बत नहीं थी। It gives you aesthetics. उसके अंदर — अंग्रेज़ी मे जिसे आप pleasure कहते हैं, जिसे ecstasy कहते हैं ... ecstasy in itself is a kind of pain. इसकी शक्लें बदलती रहती है, इसकी सूरत बदलती रहती है। आपकी सारी उपज उस दर्द से होती है।

"What about the pain of separation or जुदाई — उसमे भी तो pleasure ही है एक तरह का?" — I probe, wondering where it will take us.

> है तो सही। है तो सही। और वो ज़िंदगी के दर्द हैं। मैं यूँ कहूँ अगर — 'कि ख़ून निकले तो ज़ख्म लगती है, वर्ना हर चोट नज़्म लगती है'। जो लगेगी तो वो नज़्म हो जाएगी. ज़ख्म तो तब होता है जब physical हो — जो अंदर की चोट है, वो नज़्म होती है।

He does not glorify pain and adversities but dignifies it as an elixir of life and a big generative force of the pen. He says: वेदना में एक शक्ति होती है जो दृष्टि देती है, दर्द होता है तो creation भी होती है।

A selection of *nazms* is presented here that convey the cathartic effects of writing our heartaches and despairs. "A poet should be so crafty with words that he is envied even for his pains," Criss Jami's words ring true when we get awed by how Gulzar sublimates his pains into poetry:

आओ फिर नज़्म कहें
फिर किसी दर्द को सहलाके सजा ले आँखें
फिर किसी दुखती हुई रग से छुपा दें नश्तर
या किसी भूली हुई राह पे मुड़कर इक बार
नाम लेकर किसी हमनाम को आवाज़ ही दे लें

फिर कोई नज़्म कहें (*Pukhraj*, p 73)

एक नन्ही-सी नज़्म मेरे सामने आकर
मुझसे कहती है मेरा हाथ पकड़कर, "मेरे शायर'
ला, मेरे कंधो पे रख दे, मैं तेरा बोझ उठा लूँ" (*Pukhraj*, p 52)

बहुत दिन मैं तुम्हारे दर्द को सीने पे लेकर
जीभ कटवाता रहा हूँ
उसे शिव की तरह लेकर गले में,
सारी पृथ्वी घूम आया हूँ
कई युग जाग कर काटे हैं मैंने!...
...तुम्हारा दर्द दाख़िल हो चुका अब नज़्म में, और सो गया है
पुराने सांप को आख़िर अँधेरे बिल में जाके नींद आयी!! (*Pluto*, p 19)

Agonies of the heart can indeed become a powerful muse for the pen, carrying such generative sagacity that writers might want to nurture their heartaches! This is what Gulzar writes about such wilful nurturing of his pain:

दर्द में जावदानी का एहसास था
हमने लाडों से पाली ख़लिश सीने की (*Yaar Julahe*, 167)

ज़ख्म कहते हैं दिल का गहना है
दर्द दिल का लिबास होता है (*Yaar Julahe*, 161)

दिल में कुछ यूँ संभालता हूँ ग़म
जैसे ज़ेवर संभालता है कोई

अजीब हैं दिल के दर्द यारों, न हो तो मुश्किल है जीना इसका
जो हो तो हर दर्द एक हीरा, हर एक ग़म है नगीना इसका (*Ghulami*, 1985 Film)

जीने के लिए सोचा ही नहीं दर्द सँभालने होंगे (*Masoom*, 1983 Film)

Writing about pain is not only cathartic but indispensable to unveil a writer's true identity. Words of Faiz and Gulzar converge on this essence of pain:

मेरा दर्द नग़मा-ए-बेसदा	ये शायर जनम से जो साथ है मेरे
मेरी ज़ात ज़र्रा-ए-बेनिशां	इसी ने चांदनी की रेत भर भरके मेरे सीने में डाली है
मेरे दर्द को जो ज़बां मिले	हमेशा ज़िन्दगी से दर्द चुन-चुनकर मेरी आँखों पे मारे हैं...
मुझे अपना नाम-ओ-निशां मिले	...यही कहता था मुझको, 'दर्द से पहचान मिलती है'
	(*Pukhraj*, p 65)

The process of articulating our past and pains can unlock access to higher fertile grounds for the seeds of inner transformation and creativity. Gulzar's words on confronting these transformative forces are indeed profound, emotionally raw accounts that are far more persuasive for aspiring writers than any dry precepts on 'great habits of a good writer.'

THE INCUBATION PERIOD

ये सब मंझेंगी, ये सब कच्ची हैं
ये मँझती रहती हैं, बहुत बहुत वक़्त लगता है

The time-period for the nourishing, the *parvarish*, is indispensable to the process of literature. Gulzar has written and spoken passionately about the importance of an incubation period in the creative process and the persistence it demands.

> ज़िन्दगी में 'ऊला' कैफ़ियत से गुज़रते रहते हैं और सानी की गिरह देर तक नहीं लगती। (*Kuch aur Nazmein*)

> कभी कभी कुछ नज़्मों से यूँ होता है
> वक़्त अगर न सीचें तो वो सूखने लगती हैं
> अल्फ़ाज़ भी मुरझाकर मिसरों पर खुलने लगते हैं
> रंग उतर जाते हैं उनके,
> नज़्म किसी बीते मौसम के पत्ते जैसी उड़ती रहती हैं!! (*Pluto*, p 79)

Reading and hearing Gulzar reveal that the incubation or '*manjhna*' is as much about the intuitive nourishment that takes place in the infiniteness of mind, as it is about the deliberate, enduring effort of polishing a thought.

Before a beautiful string of words of a '*manjhee*' poetry can give an aesthetic rush to a reader, the writer has to endure a complete cycle of converting the inherent difficulties, contradictions, dilemmas into a moment of beauty and truth — doing so with an economy of words and emotions, and eloquence. Gulzar writes about this arduous process in *Kirche* and *Portrait of a Poet*:

> टुकड़ा इक नज़्म का
> दिन भर मेरी सांसों में सरकता ही रहा
> लब पे आया तो ज़बां कटने लगी
> दांत से पकड़ा तो लब छिलने लगे
> ना तो फेंका ही गया मुँह से, ना निगला ही गया
> कांच का टुकड़ा अटक जाए हलक़ में जैसे
> टुकड़ा वो नज़्म का सांसों में सरकता ही रहा (*Pukhraj*, p 114)

तूत की शाख़ पे बैठा कोई
बुनता है रेशम के तागे
लम्हा-लम्हा खोल रहा है
पत्ता-पत्ता बीन रहा है
एक-एक सांस बजाकर सुनता है सौदाई
एक-एक सांस को खोलके अपने तन पर लिपटाता जाता है (*Pukhraj*, p 167)

The two essential elements of this incubation period that Gulzar has talked about are: bringing brevity and adding a new dimension to the creative expression.

BRING BREVITY AND MINIMALISM

कम लिखने में ज़्यादा तअस्सुर है

इक नज़्म का मिसरा कसते हुए
अलफ़ाज़ के जंगल में घुस कर
मख़्सूस कोई मानी जब तोड़ के लाता हूँ... (*Neglected Poems*, p 114)

Gulzar considers bringing brevity to be paramount to the potency of poetry:

> The moment you start talking too much, people stop listening to you. Anything over-said reduces the impact and becomes prosaic. A few words are more powerful and effective. Through my poetry, I try to convey important things, which are complete in their own way.

His advice is to make each word complete — full and fecund! Selected *nazms* are shared here where Gulzar has described the elegant process of bringing brevity:

इक नज़्म का मिसरा कसते हुए
अलफ़ाज़ के जंगल में घुस कर

मख़्सूस कोई मानी जब तोड़ के लाता हूँ
हाथों पे ख़राशें पड़ती हैं
और उँगलियाँ छिल जाती हैं मगर
वो लफ्ज़ ज़ुबान पे रखते ही
मुंह में इक रस घुल जाता है (*Neglected Poems*, p 114)

इक ख़्याल को काग़ज़ पे दफनाया तो
इक नज़्म ने आँखें खोल के देखा
ढेरों लफ़्ज़ों के नीचे वो दबी हुई थी
सहमी सी, इक मद्धम सी, आवाज़ की भाप
उडी कानों तक
क्यों इतने लफ़्ज़ों में मुझको चुनते हो?
बाहें कस दी हैं मिसरों की
तशबीहों के पर्दों में हर जुम्बिश तह कर देते हो
इतनी ईंटें लगती हैं क्या एक ख़्याल दफ़नाने में?! (*Neglected Poem*, p 128)

A favorite example of brevity of expression is the *nazm* below where expectant silence speaks of a labyrinth of issues:

सूरज की इस बैक-लाइट में,
घर के खंडहर ...
और दीवारों पर बैठे,
अफ़ग़ानी बच्चे
अमेरिका के 'आर्ट जर्नल के' 'कवर पेज' पर
अब भी ज़िंदा लगते है!

हल्का हल्का धुआं निकलता रहता है (*Pandhra panch pichatar*, p 37)

ADDING AN EXTRA DIMENSION OR MYSTERY TO POETRY

खिड़की खोल दूँ, इक सतह और रख दूँ

Inseparable to the incubation and *maanjhna* is another creative practice that the Moonsmith has enthusiastically shared insights on — the adding of an extra dimension to the poetry or a 'window' to enable more layers of mystery, meaning, and a more inclusive range, as these lines convey:

> उसे मुग़ालता है मैं
> उसी की जुस्तजू में हूँ
> मुझे ये शक़ है, वो कहीं
> वो न हो, जो मुझ से छुपता फिरता है। (*Neglected Poems*, p10)

It is that latent dimension that demands de-coding and un-layering, and it is in the degree and time of engagement to uncover it that gives literature its aesthetics and magnetism. Endorsing the importance of this, Gulzar says:

> शेर जो आपके अंदर पैदा होता है एक personal moment से, उसकी एक परत खोल के dimension दे देना उसको — that's what makes it literature. That dimension that requires time to absorb it all.
>
> नज़्मों में संकेतों के अलावा बहुत कुछ मतलब हो सकते हैं। 'हाथ छुटे भी तो रिश्तें नहीं तोडा करतें' ये आप किसी रिश्ते को लगाकर देखिये या पाकिस्तान से जोड़कर देखिये। उसके मायने बदल जाते हैं। एक निजी पल के लिए लिखी गयी नज़्म को अगर यूं अस्तर जोड़ा जाय तो उसका दायरा ही बदल जाता है।

As though a poetic scientist is adding a molecule of 'effective surprise' that gets activated when it collides with the readers! And this phenomenon makes poetry timeless.

In our 2019 conversation, the Moonsmith elaborates on how such a dimension bestows creativity the virtue of transcending time and eras:

> ...शेर उतनी देर तक ज़िंदा रहेगा जब तक उस के अंदर उतनी जान है कि वो कितने ज़ाविये (angles) से सूरज की किरन पकड़ सकता है। जब तक उसमे वो diamond है, उस ख़्याल में अगर उतनी depth है कि जहाँ-जहाँ से भी किरन पकड़ ले, तो उतने उसमे और ज़ाविये हैं - तो वो ज़िंदा रहेगा, और वो बदलता रहेगा। जिस दिन वो बंद हो जायेगा – उस दिन it will start dying. इसलिए हर किसी का

ख़्याल उतनी सदी नहीं जाता जितना Shakespere का गया है, या जितना ग़ालिब जाता है।

IMPORTANCE OF A STEADY WRITING REGIME

दुकान पे रोज़ बैठता हूँ

I do not have to report to anyone and yet every day I sit with my pen and paper as if I am a clerk.

A master craftsman with a remarkably glorious career spanning over five decades continues his steady writing regime every day. He shares this discipline and work ethic with other legendary writers including E.B. White, who once said: "A writer who waits for ideal conditions under which to work will die without putting a word on paper."

The discipline and repetition of the creative process are fundamental to the मांजना and मांझना. Gulzar says: "Multiple mediums are tried including painting before you create your innate expression. Clay handle करते करते, it can lead you to be a sculptor. Passing through the process of life, it becomes your medium."

Haruki Murakami calls the repetition of the process 'a form of mesmerism' to 'reach a deeper state of mind.'

In *Boskiyana*, in response to my naïve question 'Daily *Likhte hain*?' — he chuckles and, in his unique endearing style, likens steady creative regime to the daily chores of a sweetshop:

हम्मम ... मतलब ... काम काज़ ... मेरा धंधा! दुकान पे रोज़ बैठता हूँ. कभी कुछ बिकता है कभी कुछ नहीं बिकता। ताज़ा ताज़ा लड्डू तो बनाने पढ़ते हैं शायद कोई ग्राहक आ जाये। दही रोज़ जमानी पढ़ती है, शायद कोई चला आये ... हलवाई की दुकान पे। तो दूध भी रोज़ काढ़ना पड़ता है।

For Gulzar, "Writing is not a compulsion — it is a profession and a craft. One should master the profession one practices." (*Jiya Jale,* p55)

In concluding this chapter, here is an excerpt of *nazm Guftgu* that speaks of the same self-transcendence that Gulzar referred to when he said, 'To create literature you have to live in a cave ... and that cave is nothing but you.'

... मुझे ये एहसास हो रहा है
जब उन को तक़्लीफ़ दे रहा था
वो मुझ को तक़्लीफ़ दे रही थीं! (*Raat Pashmine ki*, p 97)

MAUT MUNSIF HAI — GULZAR ON THE NATURE OF DEATH

Countless suitcases and carry bags of myriad shapes and sizes disappear into the dark tunnel, to reappear from the other side of the conveyor belt. I am at Sydney airport carousel bays waiting for my baggage. Watching the conveyor belt go around is dizzying. My father has departed from this world after four months of gruelling illness — never to return. I am back to living my life in Sydney, pondering about *karmic* cycles and *samsara*, about the human body's fragilities and rooh's eternalness. Will we meet again? The following lines are resonating in me...

...फिर कोई दायरा है
खींच ही लाता है इन्हे
जिस्म पिसते भी हैं, कट जाते हैं, मिट जाते हैं
एक ये रूह है मिटती नहीं, कटती भी नहीं

Death is a certainty yet carrying countless unknowns. One poem that conveys the finality and abruptness of death in a hard-headed way is '*Aao Na*' — that always lands in me with utmost gravity and that, despite its inherent disconsolateness, has brought much consolation during my father's health ordeal, and mother-in-law and father-in-law's passing before that:

...अमां सीने की वो ख़लिश गयी
बेक़रारियाँ, बीमारियां गयीं...

Orbiting the Moonsmith Gulzar captured his potent writings on the nature of death. This chapter presents them.

अमां सीने की वो ख़लिश गयी
बेक़रारियाँ, बीमारियां गयीं
सो भी जाओ...
सब्र ले लो
कब्र ले लो (*Haider*, 2014 Film)

"Now that life of theirs is dead and gone...," Marcus Aurelius said about the repetitive, incessant cycle of each era of — "... marrying, raising children, falling ill, dying, wars, holiday feasts, commerce, farming, flattering, pretending, suspecting, scheming, praying that others die, grumbling over one's lot, falling in love, amassing fortunes, lusting after office and power..."

Now that life of theirs is dead and gone, life's 'calendar' will still flap and flutter tomorrow — only they will not be there: मैं जो 'हूँ', 'था' हो चुका हूँगा! (*Pukhraj, p104*)

कल कलेंडर में जब सुबह होगी
"मैं कहीं नहीं हूँगा
मैं जो 'हूँ'
'था' हो चुका हूँगा"

The finality, unambiguity, and abruptness that death brings have never been put with a more hard-heartedness and no-nonsense view than in Gulzar's noir ode to death — *Aao Na* from Film Haider. A stirringly bare poetic expression of death, *Aao Na* poignantly and bluntly brings together its pathological and philosophical constructs:

बड़ा काम था उस ज़मीन पर
वो जो लिख दिया ज़बीन पर
जो गुज़र गयी, वो गुज़र गयी
बेवजह यहां, ना रहो मियाँ
चलो मियाँ, सब्र ले लो
क़ब्र ले लो

Gulzar has written powerfully about death's even-handedness, its flawlessness, and the ultimate truth it signifies. His views on the nature of death are explored in this last chapter.

TO LEARN TO DIE IS TO LEARN TO LIVE

The other side of the same coin — death assigns significance to life and a certain dignity and elegance to living. Gulzar has reminded in myriad ways that the knowing of death can focus us on being alive.

Making a persuasive case for authentic existence, he asserts that *zinda rahna* is not just about inhabiting the world but living life with fullness:

ज़िन्दगी बड़ी होनी चाहिए, लम्बी नहीं...

In our allotted lifespan, are we open to new experiences, to take risks, to love deeply, to create wholeheartedly, to connect, and to enchant? Only such peak experiences can add expanse and depth, instead of length, to our lifespan! In Boskiyana, he offers this panacea:

> Keep your antennas open ... क्योंकि कोई लम्हा नहीं है जो ज़िंदगी आपको छूके ना गुज़रती हो। It's up to you, how many of them can you capture.

With rare tact and poise, in the following *triveni,* Gulzar warns us about that state of non-aliveness that often alights upon us with its nimble feet before death's actual assigned time ... a kind of 'death before death'.

ज़िंन्दगी क्या है जानने के लिए
ज़िंदा रहना बहुत ज़रूरी है

आज तक कोई भी रहा तो नहीं (*Raat Pashmine Ki,* p 190)

In the two *nazms* below, Gulzar has depicted the flesh and bones of what it means to 'be alive' when we are alive, and not to die a premature death before we die. He speaks of the pathological and emotional conditions of such a state of non-existence, non-aliveness... 'death' before death:

दर्द हैं कोई, ना हसरत है, ना ग़म है,
मुस्कराहट की अलामत है ना कोई आह का नुक़्ता...
ना निगाहों की तहरीर ना आवाज़ का क़तरा...
कब्र में क्या दफ़न करने जा रहे हो?
सिर्फ मिट्टी है ये मिट्टी (*Raat Pashmine Ki,* p 89)

कैसे चुपचाप ही मर जाते है कुछ लोग यहाँ
जिस्म की ठंडी सी
तारिक़ सियाह कब्र के अंदर
ना किसी साँस की आवाज़
ना सिसकी कोई
ना कोई आह, ना जुम्बिश
ना ही आहट कोई
ऐसे चुपचाप ही मर जाते है कुछ लोग यहाँ
उनको दफ़नाने की ज़हमत भी उठानी नहीं पड़ती (*Pukhraj,* p 32)

A life that denies courage and connection, perceptivity and perspectives, meandering and marvelling is not alive! Gulzar's imagery of '*pilpile lamhe*' is revisited here to further examine this. Discussed in detail in the chapter about Time, *pilpile lamhe* speak to a state of vitality or fullness in experiencing moments — in contrast with the mediocre, stale, routine moments that our habituated minds experience and that he has portrayed in *nazm Aadat*:

> सांस लेना भी कैसी आदत है
> जिए जाना भी क्या रवायत है
> कोई आहट नहीं बदन में कहीं
> कोई साया नहीं है आँखों में
> पांव बेहिस हैं चलते जाते हैं
> आदतें भी अजीब होती हैं (*Pukhraj*, p 84)

Only a life lived wholly and consciously, and not habitually, can dignify the finitude of death, and gracefully embrace its ultimate truth. As Sherwin Nuland (1995) said, "The greatest dignity to be found in death is the dignity of the life that preceded it."

Gulzar unequivocally affirms that only through the experience of *pilpile lamhe*, *kaal* can be conquered and death can truly be granted a place as 'life's other half':

> ...काल चला तुमने और मेरी जानिब देखा,
> मैने काल को तोड़ कर लम्हा-लम्हा जीना सीख लिया
> पूरे का पूरा आकाश घुमा कर अब तुम देखो बाज़ी (*Yaar Julahe*, p 61)

But sadly, the aliveness of *pilpile lamhe* is not equally granted to all. *Zindagi sab pe nahin aati* — these words of Gulzar pose a vital question of life and death and bring out another defining characteristic of death. What is that? The next section takes it up.

DEATH IS NON-DISCRIMINATORY

ज़िन्दगी सब पे क्यों नहीं आती?

When we remain oblivious to the vibrancy of life that brushes past us every moment, it is a huge loss. Not everyone who is allotted *zindagi* is equally alive!

Death, on the other hand, is never lost on us — it is *munsif*, judicial, equitable — dealt even-handedly like the existential dimensions of time and space. In a masterstroke, Gulzar says:

सब पे आती है, सबकी बारी से
मौत मुन्सिफ है, कम-ओ-बेश नहीं

ज़िन्दगी सब पे क्यों नहीं आती? (Pukhraj, p 146)

These three lines and the summing-up question at the end are Gulzar's great contribution to the intriguing equation between life and death. That death is non-discriminatory, even-handed, a great leveller of life and its pathological conditions — unlike life!

ये सब खाती है...
कोई जात है इस मौत की,
ना धरम है कोई!! (*Pluto*, p 44)

क्या पता कब, कहाँ से मारेगी,
बस कि मैं ज़िन्दगी से डरता हूँ

मौत का क्या है, एक बार मारेगी (*Pukhraj*, p 145)

In the following celebrated words Gulzar refers to death as a poetic promise for all — without discernment:

मौत तू एक कविता है
मुझसे इक नज़्म का वादा है, मिलेगी मुझको
डूबती नब्ज़ों में जब दर्द को नींद आने लगे
ज़र्द-सा चेहरा लिये चांद उफ़क़ तक पहुँचे
दिन अभी पानी में हो, रात किनारे के करीब

न अंधेरा न उजाला हो, न ये रात न दिन

जिस्म जब ख़त्म हो और रूह को जब साँस आऐ
मुझसे एक नज़्म का वादा है, मिलेगी मुझको (*Pukhraj*, p 67)

DEATH — THE ULTIMATE FREEDOM

Taking the poetic promise of '*maut tu ik kavita hai*' to the next level, Gulzar has also penned death as that which is boundless and the most pious — the ultimate liberation for *rooh* from the physicality of *jism*... जिस्म जब ख़त्म हो और रूह को जब साँस आऐ...

उठाये फिरते थे एहसान जिस्म का जां पर,
चले जहाँ से तो ये पैरहन उतार चले (*Yaar Julaahe*, p163)

He elegantly reminds us that in the face of our lifelong quest to defy death and to bring order to the continuous dis-ordering of our bodies, it is death itself that will offer the ultimate freedom to the soul:

ज़रा सी देर आँखें बंद कर लो
'टनल' इक आने वाली है
जब उसके पार निकलोगे
तुम्हारा जिस्म रह जायेगा पीछे
नयी इक रौशनी से ऐसे चुन्धयायेंगी आँखें
ये आँखें खोलने की फिर ज़रुरत भी नहीं होगी! (*Pluto*, p 70)

अमां सीने की वो ख़लिश गयी
बेक़रारियाँ, बीमारियां गयीं
सो भी जाओ...
सब्र ले लो, कब्र ले लो

Liberating us from all our tussles with pain and disease, life's triumphs, and disasters, and from 'the world of hoarded wealth and certified creeds' is what death can do with dexterity. And hence, Gulzar appeals the following:

अभी यहीं थे
अभी नहीं हो
ख़्याल रखना की ज़िन्दगी की कोई भी सिलवट,
ना मौत के पाक साफ़ चेहरे के साथ जाए (*Pukhraj*, p 80)

These lines from the *nazm Pakeezah* refer to death as that which transcends beyond the convoluted-creased physicalities of life. It is that which is pious and free of all ropes: of social conditioning, of likes-dislikes, of thought-cycles, of the judgement of right and wrong, free of restlessness, worries, fear, free of all bondages:

वो जो सांस की इक फाँस थी
वो निकल गयी जो ख़राश थी

It is that blissful state of ultimate freedom when no more ensnaring breaths will hold us slave to the 'ropes' of the *Samsara*. Death is a state that Gibran defines as: "to the soul, it is the start, the triumph of life"; and a state that Gulzar promises to be as elevating as a graceful poem:

जिस्म जब ख़त्म हो और रूह को जब साँस आऐ
मुझसे एक नज़्म का वादा है, मिलेगी मुझको (*Pukhraj*, p 67)

Gulzar has also presented allegories such as *kirdaar*, *parda*, *mujrim roohein*, *daayra* — remarking on *Rooh's* tiresome *karmic* cycle of rebirth. In my 2019 *guftgu* with him, I ask him about the essence behind his *nazm Roohein*:

वक़्त के पहिये से बाँधी हुई मुजरिम रूहें
हर दफ़ा पिस के ही उठती हैं ज़मीन से लेकिन
हर दफ़ा लौट के आ जाती हैं पिसने के लिए
फिर कोई दायरा है

खींच ही लाता है इन्हे
जिस्म पिसते भी हैं, कट जाते हैं, मिट जाते हैं
एक ये रूह है मिटती नहीं, कटती भी नहीं (*Pukhraj*, p 76)

'यहाँ आप karmic cycle की बात कर रहे हैं?,' I ask him. Wielding the elegant imagery of 'the wheel,' he explains:

> The wheel! It is the wheel — पूरा! आप ऊपर चले जाते हैं, और फिर नीचे आ रहे हैं, and it goes on. You are tied up, bonded with that. You are studded into that wheel of time. और वो घूमता रहेगा ... the human races keep on perishing and going up and down.
>
> अभी ना पर्दा गिराओ ठहरो की दास्तान आगे और भी है
> अभी तो टूटी है कच्ची मिट्टी अभी तो बस जिस्म ही गिरे हैं
> अभी तो किरदार ही बुझे हैं
> अभी सुलगते हैं रूह के ग़म अभी धडकते हैं दर्द दिल के
> अभी तो एहसास जी रहा है
>
> यहीं से उठेगा कोई किरदार फिर इसी रोशनी को लेकर
> कहीं तो अंजाम ओ जुस्तजू के सिरे मिलेंगे
> अभी न पर्दा गिराओ ठहरो
>
> जिस्म ख़त्म हो गए ... what remained is the soul — the wheel of the soul is still going on. The generations have not come to an end — वो आज भी हैं। वो सिर्फ़ physical presence हैं जो ख़त्म हो जाती है, कट जाती है, मरती है, चली गयी — but the wheel is still full of it.
>
> उसमे वो जो continuity है जो आपकी चले ही जा रही है ... बाकी तो उसके ऊपर जिस्म आते हैं, चले जाते हैं ...
>
> रूह बचा ली
> ना कटी ना मिटी
> लेकिन फिर से वक़्त के
> काल के जाल में आएगी

Again, quoting the same scientist — and some of his colleagues also, whom I have read — Hinduism is the first religion that mentioned '*Awaagaman.*' It is not mentioned in Egypt, Greece, or China — the three oldest civilisations. It is only Hinduism, which says that you will be born again. But when Hinduism says reborn, it means life will not die, life will be reborn. It does not mean that Gopal Das died and Gopal Das will be reborn. It is the gene that does not die! It is the life that does not die. ये फिर पैदा हो जाएगी, ये किसी और shape में आएगी। आज अगर वो insect की सूरत में शुरू हुई थी तो अगले दफ़ा किसी पत्ते से फिर शुरू हो सकती है। Life will not die. Life will be reborn, even if it perishes. It's like *ghaas* in that poem of mine..."

कई फुट बर्फ़ के नीचे भी लेकिन
घास अपने बीज लेकर ज़िंदा रहती है...

वो कहीं से इक दरार में से इक जगह निकली — सीलन आ गयी, वहां से फिर एक पत्ती निकल आयी... once again it will start the process. That is the life that will not die. It is the life, not the individual, that will not die.

In concluding this chapter, here is an excerpt from *nazm Mausam* that poignantly reminds us of what Sherwin B. Nuland (1995) said, "We die so that the world may continue to live." Indeed, the generative markings of the bygone generations are vital for the flourishing of the forthcoming generations...

ग़ौर से देखना बहारों में
पिछले मौसम के भी निशां होंगे (*Pukhraj*, p 64)

IN CONVERSATION WITH GULZAR

22 April 2019 | *Boskiyana*, Mumbai

The conversation with Gulzar Saab is an antidote to my continued puzzlement about some of the complexities and challenges of modern humanity such as the inaction on climate change, human hand in all this, and the pervasiveness of artificial intelligence and technology in our lives. His strong hold on the swiftly shifting sands of times, and the history of civilisation, is exactly what we need to hear to combat the growing culture of insecurities, excessive entitlements, and damaging apathy.

Photo: Samit Chandra

SHAILJA CHANDRA

I believe that we are at an important point in the timeline of humanity when we are generally doing well as a civilisation. Hamari life expectancy badh gayi ha, beemariyan kam hain ... gareebi thodi kam hai ... overall, the world is relatively better-off.

Lekin kuch aise mudde hain jo hamen pareshaan kar rahe hain ... specially scientists ko. We often look at our existence from the perspective of humans, but if we looked at our existence from the angle of other, non-human, species, we could see that humans have driven the planet and some species to the brink of extinction:

GULZAR

Non-human se matlab kya hai?

SHAILJA

Ped-paudhe, jeev-jantu ... hamaare oceans, hamaare jungles ...

GULZAR

Bilkul theek hai

SHAILJA

Aapka perspective hamesha layered hota hai, aur jab bhi dobara sunen to kuchh nayi insights milti hain. So, I wanted to hear your views on the issue of global warming and environmental degradation…

GULZAR

Hum jabaani baat kar sakte hain, lekin maine express kiya hai apne aap ko — how I feel about the environment and my rapport with the trees, with the leaves, with their colours.

SHAILJA

Ji, Green poems me wo sab hai.

GULZAR

Khaas tuar se Green Poems ke naam se ik poori kitaab hai is bare me.

Jungle ka — environment ke saath — apna ek desh hai, jaise chal raha hai. Haina.

Lekin dheere dheere se jab jungle se pagdandiyan paanv nikaalne lagti hain tou pedon ke andaaz badalne lagte hain. Pedon ko samajh me aane lagta hai ki ye pagdandiyan, ye jo yahan se nikal rahi hain matlab — ye insaan yahan tak aane lag gaya — basti banegi. Ek nazm hai jisme isko bayaan kiya hai maine.

Aur ab basti banegi tou ye yaad rakho, hum me se bahut se hain jo nahin rahne waale. Un pedon ko khabar hai is baat ki. Aur wo ye bhi jaante hain ki ye pagdandi kitni chouri ho gayi hai, aur hame kuchh road-rollers ki aawazein aane lagi hain. Katne ke din qareeb hain, katne ke din qareeb hain. Un pedon ko pataa hai...

Aur ye nahin hai ki parindo ko nahin maloom, wo bhi jaante hain. Kyonki aas-paas bastiyan jab nazar aane lagti hain, log nazar aane lagte hain, jyada aane lagte hain, tou unhe maloom hain ki ye insaan jo aa raha hai ye yahan pe kuchh na kuchh karega.

Tou ye environment hai! Hum jab non-humans ki baat karte hain tou non-humans are aware of it. Sirf ye hain ki human beings are too dominant. Kya kahen — dictators hain (laughs).

Unki hukumat chalti hai tou wo pedon ko aur environment ko ghulam banaaye rakhte hain.

Tou mushkil hoti hai, but they do react to it. Kal ki ya parson ki bhi khabar thi, uske aage bhi thi — ki school ke andar leopard milaa. Wo jaa ke andar baitha hua tha aaraam se.

Aur, kal hi ke paper ki khabar hai, ki jhopdi ke baahar sone waali ek aurat ki aankh khuli tou tiger, big cat, ka moonh khula hua tha bachhe ke sir ke upar — wo chhota sa bachha, jo soa hua tha. Jaisa likha hai khabar me. Aur, is aurat ne thapad maara tiger ko. Tiger is ki taraf jhapka, wo chillai aur wo bhaag gaya.

She saved the child — jahan se koi bachne ki ummeed nahin thi. Ek minute pahle agar uski aankh nahin khulti tou — can you imagine what would have happened?

Tou aisa nahin ki wo humein maarne aate the, hum unhe maarne jaaya karte the.

SHAILJA

Unka habitat humne badal diya...

GULZAR

Shikaar karne hum jaaya karte the, jaanwar nahin jaaya karte the shikaar karne.

Lekin aapne unke jungle kaat diye, unke rahne ki jagah kaat dee. Rocks me bhi agar rahte the, tou aapne unko khod kar wahan se cement bana liya, patthar nikal liye, aur aapne immaratein banaani shuru kar dee. Tou kahan jaayenge wo? So, this co-existence is vanishing — this coexistence with humans. Jise aap non-humans kah rahe hain, mujhe wo human lagte hain.

SHAILJA

Ji, aapke saare portrayals me unka hi 'point of view' dikhaya gaya hai...

GULZAR

Green Poems is lihaaz se padhne ke qaabil hai. I want this generation and children to know what environment is and why it is important to preserve our environment. Taaki unhe maloom hota rahe ki shakhon pe patte aate hain, tou ek rang aata hai, rang aaten hain tou phool aa jaate hain. Tou lagta hai ki ped kuchh likh raha hai.

SHAILJA

Ungliyan dubo ke dhoop me… aapne likha tha…

GULZAR

Haan. Shakhen yun nikalti hain jaise ped ne lakeerein kheenchi hain, uske upar kuch likhna hai. Aur uske upar patton ke hurruf aane lagte hain, aur maatraayen aati hain phoolon ki. Aur unke rang, unki drawing aati hain — aur saare aate hain. Wo sajaaye rakhte hain ped apne. It dresses up very well!

Aur, hum ko ye hai ki — jahan koi mehkaa, khilaa, aur uski gardan kaat kar guldaan me lagaa dee. Tou, I have expressed myself about the environment.

SHAILJA

Green Poems is a beautiful anthology. Soil aur Society par jo Chapter hai, wo aapki Green Poems ko hi explore karta hai.

Sustainability ke subjects par lecture karti hoon tou main zyada jazbaati hoon shayad — but Global Warming, I believe, is a real threat.

Scientists believe that humans have been reckless and that our progress is achieved at the expense of the planet and its natural habitats. That earth's climate change is real, and as a result half of all species alive today could disappear over the next century. Global warming could make some parts of the world unthinkably uninhabitable or unable to produce the food and resources that we require for sustenance. That our ocean levels will rise, the coral reef will get rapidly bleached, fishes will drown in plastic rubbish. They believe that there is a strong human hand in all this. It is a result of our actions or inactions.

But then there are some other scientists who think differently — who believe that our nature and ecosystem is so resilient — unlike humans — and hence fishes, birds, trees, oceans are merely 'observing' these changes and these species will be able to reverse the adverse effects of damaging changes. So, I find it really intriguing. Aur mujhe lagta hai ki humans shayad rahenge nahin ye dekhne ke liye ki waqai hamara ecosystem itnaa resilient hai ki nahin hai!

GULZAR

Jis tarah aap society ko environment ke saath dekh rahe hain, environment ko poore globe ke saath dekhiye. Aur is globe ko poori qaynaat ke saath dekhiye.

Kyonki ye yahan pe khatm nahin hone walaa hai.

Well, you are related to your Milkyway galaxy, and your galaxy is again related to the further spaces and further galaxies and further solar systems — and not one, there are many!

Matlab aap baat sochen tou khyaal aur soch se baahar ho jaata hai. That they are beyond which you can't even think, as Carl Sagan says — ki human being is limited in its thinking because it can only think to a certain extent.

Insaan jo sochta hai usko wo kar lega. Kyonki wo impossible soch hi nahin sakta. Sochta wahi hai jo possibility me hai. That is a limitation of human beings, that you can't think impossible.

Jo soch rahen hai wo aapki iss genetic growth me possible hai — only then you can think of it.

Agar aap Arabian Nights se leke baat karen — tou globe rakha, aur prince kahan jaa raha hai, main dekhta hoon, main bataata hoon kahan hai! Now the TV is there — the expression was different. And how long? Hardly 2000 years back.

Your life is the life of the globe — the life of the gene and the life of the life itself. This is also billions of years back. Tou, 2000 saal tou jeb ke chane ki tarah hain, kuchh bhi nahin hain. Tou, wahan (climate change) pe jab aap baat karte hain — it is taking a different shape. Shapes badalti jaayengi.

Aur wahan se chale hue ek ped ki shakal aaj wahin nahin hai, jahan se chale the, jahan se zindagi shuru hui thi. Panchhi waise ke waise nahin hai, haathi waise ke waise nahin hai, jaanwar waise ke waise nahin hai. Matlab agar aap purani tasveer ghode ki dekhen tou kuchh aur nazar aata hai.

Insaan ki shaql dekh len tou wo alag ho gaya hai. Haathi ki shaql dekh len tou haathi us waqt ka itnaa hairy jaanwar tha. Aaj dekhiye kya hai wo. Tou, wo to badlta rahega, aur aage bhi badalta rahega. Like the way they say that they will reverse the effects — tou wo badal lenge.

Aur badalne par kuchh nikal jaayenge kuch rah jayenge. Kuchh ki shape badal jaayegi, kuchh naye aa jayenge. Usme se paida honge.

Pedon me se agar puraane se puraana element dekhen — while I'm saying this, I'm also quoting Carl Sagan because I am very fond of his writing, one of the greatest scientists that happened in our times — tou Peepal ka ek ped hai jisme wo saare cells and molecules hain jahan se ye life paida hui thi. Abhi tak hai, har peepal ke ped me! Uske elements dawaai me isliye kaam aaye — because those were the same elements as life's molecules and cells.

Tou, usko preserve karne ki koshish me humne usko baandh diya. Ki dekho ye ped mat kaatna. Baaki tum kaat lo jo bhi lakdi ke liye kaatna hai, par ye Peepal badaa kaam aayega.

Jab phir bhi society nahin maani tou — they made religion out of a system of society. Religion aur kya hai? Rahne-sahne ka dhang jo banaa lete hain. Tou, unhone uski pooja karwaani shuru kar dee. Iske upar dhaaga baandh do, dekho ye mat kaatna kuch galat ho jayega. Tou, Peepal bachne lag gaya — one of the oldest!

I'm again quoting Carl Sagan — he has written a complete chapter on Natraj, which is worth reading in his book of Cosmos. So, one has to learn all this.

And the oldest creature, which has come from there is the cockroach, whose shape has changed very little, who can bear severest cold and severest heat. Tou, agar aap dekhen tou scientist aise bewajah nahin kah rahe hain, they are quoting something. They are telling you a process.

Process me abhi ye hai ki — you have started going to the Mars and beyond. Aap kyon talaash kar rahe hain ye jagah? Because you want to learn what is Space. Ye qaaynaat hai kya? And there is not one universe, there are many a universes. Ek universe nahin hai. Agar universe bhi ek nahin hai, bahut zyada hain — so there is an interlink somewhere, it has to happen. Wo to hoga!

8 billion years is approximately the life of the earth. Jisme se 3.6 billion bache hain — we have already travelled that much. 3.6 Billion maine zikr bhi kiya hai kisi jagah pe — kisi poem me...

SHAILJA

Ji, chaar hi billion saal bache hain

GULZAR

Haan — and that's the correct figure. Tou, agar aap ye samjhen ki ye earth permanent hai tou wo bhi nahin hai.

Because you belong to a dwarf son. Jo aapka sooraj hai — it is only a dwarf son. Is se — matlab hazaron bhi chhota lagta hai bolte hue — zayada bade sooraj hain qaaynaat me.

Tou, ye jab bujhne lagega, bujhega aur iskaa daayra failega tou sabse pahle Mercury jayega, Venus jayega, Earth jayegi — uske baad ek-ek kar ke baaki jaayenge.

Have you thought in terms of that qaaynaat? Your mind will start boggling. Jab aadmi us space ka andaaza laagaane lagtaa hai — tou, these become very minor questions then. This is the process. This is the process.

It is a process of evolution. Aur ye to chalta rahega. Agar aap samajhte hain ki ye band ho jaane wala hai, aur phir theek ho jaayega. Ye yahan par nahin rukne waala. Chalegi ye process, ye badalata rahega.

SHAILJA

What are your views on the cycle of death and rebirth? The transmigration of the aatma or the karmic cycle? Main aapki wo nazm padh rahi thi — Jism piste bhi hain, kat jaate hain, mit jaate hain, Ek ye rooh hai, mit ti nahin, kat ti bhi nahin.

GULZAR

Dekhiye, ye humne theory banaayee hui hai tassalli dene ke liye. Again, quoting the same scientist — and some of his peers also, whom I have read — Hinduism is the first religion that mentioned 'Awaa-gaman.' It is not mentioned in Egypt, Greece, or China — the three oldest civilisations. It is only Hinduism, which says that you will be born again. But when Hinduism says reborn, it means life will not die, life will be reborn. It does not mean that Gopal Das died and Gopal Das will be reborn. It is the gene that does not die! It is the life that does not die. Ye phir paida ho jayegi, ye kisi aur shape me aayegi. Aaj agar wo insect ki soorat me shuru hui thi tou agle dafaa kisi patte se phir shuru ho sakti hai. Life will not die. Life will be reborn, even if it perishes. It's like ghaas in that poem of mine..."

SHAILJA

'Kai foot barf ke neeche bhi lekin ghaas apne beej lekar zinda rahti hai...'

GULZAR

Wo kahin se ik daraar me se ik jagah nikli — seelan aa gayi, waha se phir ek patti nikal aayi. Once again it will start the process. That is the life that will not die. It is the life, not the individual, that will not die.

SHAILJA

This gives me so much hope! In my classes, I often break it down into even smaller matters such as what is carbon emissions and how it creates global warming, and several other questions that often bother me and students. But hearing the process of life, evolution and our place in the enormous cosmos — all this instills hope in me.

GULZAR

Aapne wo padhi hain — Kaal Maayi?

SHAILJA

Jee jee, thaali wali? Haanji.

GULZAR

Padhi hai na? Because if God has given birth, who has given birth to God?

Aur aapne ye kaise faisla kiya ki wo purush hai, Khuda naari kyon nahin hai?

Agar paidayish hoti hai naari se hi, maa hai – tou ye kahan se beech me aa gaya? Ki jise paida hi nahin kiya kisi ne. Ye aise hi kaise ho gaya? So, there has to be a naari behind him then.

And that is why I called that He is born of time, the infinity. He is born of the infinity, which is Kaal. Then I thought that Kaal must be a woman. Ki kaal maayi ki aawaaz hai ye. Jo baitha hua, khelta bhi rahta hai, aur thaali se gola banaa ke fenk deta hai ek, aur uske planet bana deta hai.

So must be Kaal Mayi. That is what is to be understood in those poems. Uski teen-chaar poems hain where I have talked about that — about infinity. They are not as superficial as they look like.

SHAILJA

Jee ... sach bataaun tou maine is tarah se nahin samjhi thi wo nazmein. Aur bahut kuch aur hoga aapki writings me jo main abhi nahin samjhi hoon... isliye ongoing journey hai ye.

Main ye kuchh aur nazmein padh rahi thi, usme mujhe karmic pattern ki baat lagti hai...

GULZAR

Kaun si?

SHAILJA

Rooh bachaa lee, na kati na miti,
lekin phir se waqt ke, kaal ke jaal me aayegi

And

Jism piste bhi hain, kat jaate hain, mit jaate hain
Ek ye rooh hai, mit ti nahin, kat ti bhi nahin

GULZAR

(in sync) Kat ti bhi nahin...

SHAILJA

Tou, aap yahan karmic cycle ki baat kar rahe hain — the cycle of death and rebirth?

The wheel! It is the wheel — Poora. Aap upar chale jaate hain, aur phir neeche bhi aa rahe hain, and it goes on. You are tied up, bonded with that. You are studded into that wheel of time. Aur wo ghumta rahega. The human races keep on perishing and going up and down...

Jism khatam ho gaye. What remained is the soul — the wheel of the soul is still going on. The generations have not come to an end — wo aaj bhi hain. Wo sirf physical presence hai, jo khatm ho jaati hai, kat jaati hai, marti hai, chali gayee — but the wheel is still full of it...

Usme wo jo continuity hai — that is the aatma — jo

aapki chale hi jaa rahi hai. Baaki tou uske upar jism aate hain, chale jaate hai.

SHAILJA

Is concept the same as what Carl Sagan said and you quoted earlier — Aatma life ko bhi kah sakte hain?

GULZAR

Jee haan.

SHAILJA

Computers and machines — technological dystopia ka jo darr hai humanity ko — ki technology humko hijack kar legi! Ki artificial intelligence humse jyada intelligent na ho jaaye kahin!

Of course, technology has been a great benefit for our lives, and it has helped us in keeping connected. Many problems that appeared mammoth in the past have now — thanks to comupters and internet — become so easy. But, human inventions, even with the best of intentions, can have damaging unintended consequences. I wanted your views on technology, social media and its other aspects that have become addictive and damaging and have stripped us off the charms of uncertainties and not knowing.

Aap technology ke bahut saath saath chale hain, aur uska haath nahin chhoda hai. What is your view in general about technology, and in particular Artificial Intelligence?

GULZAR

Technology aap jisko kah rahee hain — it is not a separate existence. It is you placing yourself into it — that is why it is running. It is your own extension. Jitna aap dimaag me rakh sakte the — jab wo bhar gaya hai tou baahar likh diya. Jab aap soch me yaad rakhte the, tou aahista-aahista pustak aa gayi. Aapne us me likhna shuru kar diya. So, books became the technology of that time.

Pahle patra the, tamra-patra the, phir chhaal par likhne lage. Phir usko baandhne lag gaye, phir pustak ki shakal aayi. Puskak bhi kitnaa haath se likhte, phir humne chhapayee paida kar lee.

Jab chhapaayee paida karlee tou aapne chhaapa-khaana, printing press banaa liya. Was that not technology?

That was a technology we started because of memory. Ki memory me kitna rakhenge aap? Chhaapa-khaane me karna padhta tou urdu me pahle likh ke pathhar me chhapte the — phir aapne words coin kar liye, alphabets ko arrange kar ke print karna shuru kar diya.

You have come up to this — ki aap ko na arrange karna na kuch, seedha type karne lag gaye hain.

It is not that you are doing it today — you have been doing it all along, and it will keep on changing shape.

Book se pahle aapne zabaani yaad karwana shuru kar diya tha — Sanskrit ke ye shlok bana diye, usko poetry bana diya — so that was also a technique. Taaki ye gaate raho, gaate raho. Yaad rahega tou aglee generation tak jaayega — jab wo aaye tou finally usko note karna shuru. Uske bhi words banaaye — pahle shaklon se jo samajh me aati thi. Ye sound kya hai, or wo sound kaise hai — jo aaj bhi Japanese and Chinese me istemaal ho raha hai.

Sounds se aahista-aahista humne alphabets utaar liye. Har ek ilaake ke apne-apne bane. Hebrew ne apnaa banaya jahan se English shuru hui, aur Latin ke pahle Sanskrit aur ... these are the mother tongues. Different places emerged differently, but technique started from there, not from today. It is placing yourself outside yourself, when you cannot retain anymore.

Tou, aap hi usme hain na? Aapne khud hi ko usme rakhna shuru kar diya — kyonki sab aap andar nahin absorb kar sakte — kyonki memory ke bhi there are certain number of cells. Us se jyada aap nahin store kar paate. Aur usko chhaan lena, phir dhundhna, yaad karna ki wo kya dawa batayi thi aur uske pair me dard tha, nahin angoothe pe kuchh chhaala tha. Nahin nahin, chhala nahin tha wo kuch uske andar se pus nikli thi. Saara ka saara aapne note kar liya tou Ayurvedic bana liya, medicines banaa lee.

So, this technology is you, yourself — it is not an outside entity — ki jo aapko pakad legi. Haina? It is you catching yourself. Haina?

Apkaa apna existence hai na wo? Aur technology agar intelligent ho jaayegi tou koi doosra individual tou nahin hai — it is you yourself. Haan ... tou (intelligent) ho jaayegi tou paal lijiye use...

(Laughs)... haan... I hope I am relevant to your questions?

SHAILJA

You are opening my mind to new directions!

One subject that I often think about, and perhaps no one has any answer to, is the question of our freewill and destiny. As human beings, kabhi-kabhi hamein lagta hai hum control kar rahe hain khud ki journey, decision, actions, outcomes ko. Par, aisa bhi lagta hai ki hamaare haath me kuchh nahin. Sometimes we find comfort in exercising our agency, and sometimes we find comfort in knowing that everything is destined. I wish to hear your insights.

GULZAR

Actually, I am not the right person to answer this. Aapko kisi rishi-muni ke paas baith ke poochne chahiye ye sawaal.

As a poet — I am one of those who are researching on it. Jo dhundh raha hai, talaash kar raha hai. I am one like you that is why I keep on writing it, putting it on paper. Not that I have all the answers to all this. I am only reacting to your questions because iss ki talaash mujhe bhi hai. Aur maine jahan tak talaash kiya, maine aapko bataa diya. Ho sakta hai mujhe aage kuchh aur maloom ho jaaye — is se aage bhi kuchh pataa lage.

Aur hamare haath me kya hai, matlab? Likha hua kahin se tou kuch hai nahi, ki kisi ne aapki destiny likhi hui hai. Likhne waala kaun hai? Kahan pe hai? Kaun likhega destiny?

Kisi destiny ko, likhe hue ko dhundhne ki kya zaroorat hai?

I mean we are searching unnecessary for a few things. It is actually shunning one's self. That is why you are finding it somewhere outside — ki hamaara kiya hua nahin hai, ye to destiny me tha hi. Kyonki aap apnee zimmewaari se chhoot jaate hain us se. That is where the birth of God started. Wo shuru hi wahan se hota hai. Anything unknown, anything that you do not know is God.

Matlab jis waqt ye nahin pataa tha insaan ko ki jungle me ye aag kaise lagi. They didn't know fire is an element. Us waqt insaan usko koi jaanwar samajhta tha.

Ab bijli upar se giri aur ped jalne lag gaya jungle me — ab usko maarne ki koshish kar raha hai chhadi se, tou wo chhadi me bhi aa gayi — chhadi fenk di.

Tou, jab tak aap ko nahin samajh me aaya kya hai fire, aap uski pooja karne lage — ki bhai ye tou bhagwaan hai... haina?

Jab samajh me aane laga tou pata chala ki ye tou aag hai. Shuru shuru me jab kabeele ghumte the tou — wo kabeela zayada taakatwar ho jaata tha jiske paas fire bhi hai. Tou, usko aag ko zinda rakhne ke, aur saath me lekar carry karne ke tareeke dhundhe unhone, because then you become a powerful tribe.

Tou, kaun si likhi hui destiny ki baat kar rahi hain aap? Jo samajh me aati gayi wo science hoti gayi, jo nahin samajh me aayi wo khudaayee hoti gayi.

SHAILJA CHANDRA

Ek bahut badaa body of work hai by Sam Harris — wo freewill ke bare me baat karte hain ki 'free will is an illusion.' He says, 'our wills are simply not of our own making — we do not have the freedom we think we have'. He puts a lot of emphasis on our environment and background. He implies that many a times, no matter what we do and how much value we place on freewill, we cannot change our destiny. He is a scientist actually.

GULZAR

But, har ek scientist khuda me believe karta hai — koi zaroori nahin ki wo scientist hone ki wajah khuda me believe na kare. Because Khuda — usne koi daadhi-moochh wala Khuda nahin rakkha hua banaa ke — it is the process and the unknown.

Achha agar Khuda har cheez dekhta hai, aur uski marzi ke bagair patta nahin hilta, aur uski marzi ke bagair koi panchhi nahin girtaa, tou badi boring cheez hai. Wo baithe hue patte hila raha hai.

Must be very very boring and must be bored to death of his ownself — ke patte hila raha hai, matlab hadd ho gayi.

SHAILJA

Ji aapne kaha hai is baare me kisi interview me... that I relieve Him of all this.

GULZAR

Haan. Otherwise live with your environments that he has given and carry it on further now. Usne Banaa ke de diya. You are still asking him to do everything. Do it yourself!

We are stardust — all of us. We are made of the dust which has come from the stars. Jo space me se aata hai, usi ki wajah se paani paida hua, usi ki wajah se paani me clash hoke life paida ho gayi. Usi me se cell the. It was a hydrogen-based globe — this earth, which suddnely turned overnight. Something fell again from the space and it turned into an Oxygen globe. And whatever cells were born, all died. The cells which had started behaving like life, stuck to each other in that perishment — and that created the first compound cell, which had the quality to reproduce itself and that was the beginning of life.

Aaj bhi aap cells se bani hui hain, molecules se bani hui hain — aap ka yahan se agar ye baal ukhadata hai, tou us jagah pe dobara baal hi aata hai, daant nahin aata.

You are made of those, because that cell reproduces itself.

Nakhun toota tou us jagah nakhun aayega. Kyonki wo cell apne aap ko reproduce karta hai. We human beings are made of that. Not only human beings, but entire life is also made of that.

SHAILJA

Aap pahle kah rahe the ki ye rishi-muni se poochna chaiye tha. Koi bhi question mujhe aisa nahin lagta ki maine kyon poocha. Mujhe rishi-muni se poochhna hi nahin, mujhe aapse hi poochhna hai!

GULZAR

We also ask those who are wiser than us. Matlab kahan tak hum gain kar paaye, hum pass on karte hain — kabhi likh kar, kabhi bataa kar, kabhi bol kar. Aap aage paas on karengee, zaahir hai. It is a process.

Jo nahin samajh me aata hum apne gyaniyon se poochte hain. Us me se kuch samajh me padhta hai, kuchh upar se guzarata hai sar ke.

Humse gyaani pahle bhi the, aur humse gyaani aage bhi honge. If I consider myself ki 'main bada gyaani hoon' — then I am living in a fool's paradise as they say in English ... haina (Laughs).

Ab aaapko ye nahin pata ki uske liye koi chhota bade ka sawaal nahi hai. Ab main aapse baat karte-karte kab koi baat seekh gaya aapko pataa bhi nahin lagega. Nobody teaches anyone. One only exposes one's own knowledge to others and usme se jisne seekh liya seekh liya. Sikhaya hua kisi ka bhi nahin hai.

SHAILJA

The last question. Sometimes I feel nervous to exercise my artistic or creative freedom to bring my vantage points to your words…

GULZAR

Haan, nahin, but you can! Agar Shakespere ne ya Ghalib ne jo likha tha, uska wahi matlab hota jo wo kah raha hai, tou uske reinterpretation ki kya zaroorat thi? The only thing is — usme layers hain! Usne jis zindagi ke baare me kaha hai, wo zindagi badal gayee waqt ke saath — and yet if it is the truth — wo phir paida hogi, wo phir usme jagah dhundh lega, aur wo badalta rahega — isliye reinterpretation hoti tahegi, hoti rahegi. Jisko wo jis point of view se nazar aa jaaye.

Ek hi sunset maine describe kiya — but five thousand people on the beach will see the same sunset differently. You have said this also. Everybody has the liberty to reinterpret it as they conceive it reveals to us — that it applies to my life like this."

Utni der tak wo zinda rahega jab tak us sher ke andar utni jaan hai ki wo kitne zaaviye, angles, se sooraj ki kiran pakad sakta hai. Jab tak usme wo hai, diamond jahan-jahan se bhi pakad le. Tou, us khayaal me agar utni depth hai, aur utne usme zaaviye hain, tou wo zinda rahega aur wo badalta rehega. Jis din wo band ho jayega, us din – it will start dying. Isliye har kisi ka khayaal utni sadi nahin jaata jitna Shakespere ka gaya hai, ya jitna Ghalib jaata hai.

So, there is not only one interpretation. Aap mujhse maayne poochen tou, it is not easy to explain it. I can only explain an incident but the feeling inside, which produced this couplet — it is not possible to totally explain that. Wo mumkin nahin hai.

Shailja grew up in the enchanting hills of Uttrakhand, India. Her quest for sustainability and new realms led her to Sydney, where she loves balancing her work as a radio broadcaster, sustainability consultant, and educator. Being a rapt *Musafir* of Gulzar's words is a sweet passion of her. Her last name might as well be Gulzar, as a friend once quipped. In *The Moonsmith Gulzar*, she unravels the philosophical, emotional, and existential themes in Gulzar's writings on some of the greatest preoccupations of the human mind. This is her first book.

www.ingramcontent.com/pod-product-compliance
Ingram Content Group UK Ltd.
Pitfield, Milton Keynes, MK11 3LW, UK
UKHW042017190726
13854UKWH00005B/2328

9 789391 431211